BIBLES, SCIENCE, AND SANITY

The Case for Modernism

Richard White, Ph.D.

DORRANCE PUBLISHING CO., INC.
PITTSBURGH, PENNSYLVANIA 15222

ISBN # 0-8059-6630-7
Printed in the United States of America

First Printing

For information or to order additional books, please write:
Dorrance Publishing Co., Inc.
701 Smithfield Street
Third Floor
Pittsburgh, Pennsylvania 15222-3906
U.S.A.
1-800-788-7654
Or visit our web site and on-line catalog at
www.dorrancepublishing.com

This book is dedicated to science teachers who reveal the true wonders of nature; to scientists like Frederick (Fred) E. Samson, Ph.D., and Harold E. Himwich, M.D., who make science real; and to religious leaders and other members of mankind who prize civility and reason.

CONTENTS

INTRODUCTION

THE SCIENTIFIC METHOD IS ARGUABLY THE SUPREME INVENTION OF THE MIND. It has unquestionably shaped civilization, yet few equate science with culture or use it as a way of thinking. Culture and ethnicity are commonly identified as a mix of food, dress, sports, art, music, architecture, agriculture, industry, language, mores, customs, ceremonies, superstition, government, and religion. No science is needed in this mix. Science only becomes important when there is a desire to be best informed about natural phenomena and when a society is considered modern or enlightened. History teaches, however, that many reject the findings of scientists when their findings are contrary to religious beliefs.

In America today, there is a relentless effort by Christian fundamentalists to define what is science. They have welcomed the creationists who are conversant with scientific terminology and who declare that all terrestrial life began supernaturally less than 10,000 years ago. Their account of the origins of life crudely resembles that described in Genesis but rejects the Bible as perfect science. Nevertheless, the fundamentalists have supported the creationists and together they condemn the evidence of evolution. The fundamentalists have managed to abolish the teaching of evolution by law in some states and wish to eradicate the science. On the other hand, the creationists try to have their theory of creation taught by law. Recent polls indicate that their efforts have been rewarded. One poll in the year 2000 concluded that 79 percent felt that creationism should be taught alongside evolution in public schools. Another poll in 2003 stated that 28 percent of those asked accepted evolution while 48 percent sided with creationism. As discussed in more detail later, fundamentalists are required by decree to deny any science that may overturn Scripture on creation and the flood. Students with that faith, therefore, must abandon their religion if they accept the facts of evolution. Contrary to Scripture, fundamentalists would have the Ten

Commandments, but not the Eleventh, displayed in all public buildings. On television and in print, the more vociferous ones freely demonize scientists, secular scholars, politicians, and other religions in the name of God. Some even claim that America was founded as a Christian nation and that this fact has been obscured by secular historians.

The remarkable growth of irrationalism has been a surprise to me and to many of my colleagues. I was reared in an industrial city during the 1930s when technology was equated to human progress and where able teachers taught how science was related to industry and to their lives. By the 1950s, the whole nation was aware that science was essential to our culture and to our future. There was the real threat of atomic warfare and when Sputnik I was launched by the Soviet Union on October 4, 1957, the glamour for more science education was intensified. In 1960, for the first time in our history, both presidential candidates emphasized the importance of education for the future of America. Large numbers of GIs attended college free and student loans were made available to others for higher leaning. More people attended college than ever, and it looked like the age of pure reason had arrived in the USA. It appears, however, that the science taught after WWII was more about what scientists had discovered than about the scientific method, particularly after the old-timers trained prior to 1940 vanished.

Not long ago the likes of Thomas Edison (b. 1847), Walter Reed (b. 1851), Charles Steinmetz (b. 1865), Wernher Von Braun (b. 1912) and Jonas Salk (b. 1914) were household names for their scientific studies. A building that was erected by General Electric for the 1939 New York World's Fair was named for Steinmetz sixteen years after his death. The mayor of New York then was La Guardia, and to him engineers were gods (David Gelernter, *1939: The Lost World of the Fair*, 1996). Great movies were made concerning the lives of Louis Pasteur (starring Paul Muni) and Marie Curie (starring Greer Garson), among others, that showed the essence of the scientific method. Some made medicine their career after reading best-sellers like *Arrowsmith* and *Microbe Hunters* by Paul de Kruif (published from 1926 through 1943). Popular interest in scientists, however, has waned among those born since the middle of the twentieth century. Today books about angels sell by the millions. The most likely household names in science today are Einstein and Darwin, the latter mainly because he is vilified for providing the evidence that established evolution. Perhaps the main difference between the older and younger generation is that the former experienced the changes that science and engineering brought to their lives like electricity, sky-scrapers, radios, telephones, movies, airplanes, washing machines, and immunization. Just to understand the causes of goiter, heat strokes, and pellagra were major advances prior to 1940. Even indoor plumbing was revolutionary. Scientists and engineers made living better and were heroes to most people then.

One reason why science may not play a role in the psyche of most people today is because scientific knowledge is ever expanding and requires constant study to keep abreast. Moreover, new sciences, like molecular biology, appear after some fundamental discovery which ever expands the fields of research. The fields of research are now so diverse that those expert in one field are not likely to know much of significance about another. As a consequence we must rely on the conclusions of the few trained in a given area of science. Society depends, for instance, on the expertise of the microbiologist to identify the cause of an infection and not on the astrophysicist. It is hopeless today to be an expert in all aspects of science. The only thing scientists share in their training is to be objective. Their conclusions or theories must be based on the best information available. Conclusions are therefore subject to change with new facts.

Religion need not change to accommodate new facts. It is not based on the best evidence but on beliefs that are learned as a child or that may be appealing. Religious instruction is about the supernatural, spirituality, tradition, and socializing. To some it is about influence and the power to persuade. There is no conflict between science and religion because they are entirely different forms of thought. When scientific discoveries are perceived to conflict with traditional religious belief, theologians may accept the findings and give them a religious interpretation. Thus the famous preacher Henry Ward Beecher wrote an essay in 1885 to reconcile the relatively new science of evolution with Scripture that was simply titled *Evolution and the Bible*. But today millions hold that the Bible is inerrant and, therefore, the sun may stop moving in the sky, the sun may move backwards, man may live under the water for days inside a fish, and plants and a donkey spoke—for their words are recorded. Religious dogmatists ignore such inept statements in their preaching, and to my knowledge none drink deadly things to prove they are true followers of Christ (Mark 16:18). Television has made many of them millionaires, celebrities, and political pawnbrokers. Since the 1970s they have defined for millions of people what is correct. I heard one explain why tolerance led to the full of the Roman Empire. There are, however, millions of

Americans of many faiths, who do not accept the dogma that the Bible is perfect in science and history. They are, I believe, the silent majority who may not be fully aware of the relentless assault waged by fundamentalists on our secular institutions or may be too polite to remonstrate.

In the past fifty years it has become evident that millions of our citizens, including some trained in science, will deface facts in the name of faith, denigrate science and scientists, and wish to put their faith in the face of all to see. Irrationalism is not new but its remarkable rise in our modern society is. I have documented this phenomenon and have used Scripture, news articles, and history to show how religious dogma corrupts the Bible, corrupts education, defiles reason, and was abhorred by our Founding Fathers.

CHAPTER 1

Definitions and Purpose

BIBLES: THE KING JAMES VERSION (KJV), THE REVISED STANDARD VERSION (RSV), and The Living Bible (TLB) are the Holy Books cited in this treatise. *The Illustrated Dictionary of the Bible* (Thomas Nelson Pub., 1997), *The Daily Study Bible Series* by the Scotsman William Barclay (Westminster Press), and *Halley's Bible Handbook* (Zondervan Pub. House) were consulted to help illuminate some biblical topics. The same passage taken from the different versions may have a different impact and slightly different meaning. The last passage of Mark was even deleted in one version because biblical scholars question whether it was written by the same author. It tells us that Jesus said that true believers could drink any deadly thing (KJV) and handle poisonous snakes with impunity. I have cited many such unseemly statements to refute the dogma that the Bible is inerrant in all matters, with no disrespect of our religious forefathers intended.

Science: One high school teacher took perhaps ten minutes to explain the nature of science, its methods, and how it differed from most other studies. He had an outline on the blackboard to enhance the explanation. I assumed that all students of science had similar instruction and was surprised to find out otherwise. Instead, my colleagues taught from textbooks and did research in the manner taught by mentors, oblivious to terms like emergence and inductive reasoning. More apropos, the so-called Creation scientists have declared in ignorance that evolution is not an empirical science and ignorant religious fundamentalist have declared that evolution is only a theory of false scientists. The fundamentalists also emphasize that scientific knowledge is ever changing and therefore unreliable, while statements in The

1

Book are forever certain, without error or contradiction. The beliefs of religious dogmatists and creationists are so dear to them that they advocate changing public science curricula by law to negate what they perceive to be false science. This includes Earth Science, Geology, Biology, and any scientific findings that are not compatible with biblical statements. To them the Bible determines what is science, for as Brian Edwards wrote, "an inerrant Bible submits to no man's judgment."

Science is not a sacred cow; its only altar of worship is objectivity. It does, however, share with the Boy Scouts and some religions a pledge to be honest and trustworthy. It is arguably the greatest invention of the mind for no other human endeavor has transformed the way people may live today from that of past millennia. For many science is self-rewarding and scientific knowledge has grown exponentially in nations where science is fostered. Success is measured by how well discoveries influence others devoted to the rules of objectivity. In contrast, success in religion is measured by membership and often how well its leaders influence their followers politically and economically. In many communities religion is politics, and nations that ignore science must import that knowledge if they wish to modernize. Yet in our country, some religious leaders attack science with impunity, apparently because reports indicate that most of our citizens have a poor operational understanding of the nature of science. The religious version of science that is being presented as education is corrupt. One purpose of this treatise is to demonstrate the obvious—that the Bible was never meant to be a science text nor a history text. Seth B. Hinshaw tells us that the Puritans were ever fearful that someone might be happy (*Walk Cheerfully, Friends*, 1978). The fundamentalists seem ever fearful that science might be right.

It is hoped that the discussion on the nature of science in this treatise, as well as the use of many statements from the Bible, together with facts gleaned from newspaper articles—especially *The Commercial Appeal* (CA) of Memphis—and the views of numerous writers will help students, educators, legislators, and concerned citizens to counter the fervent effects of those who would require by law that science conform to religion.

Sanity: To be of sound mind or rational is to be sane, so states the dictionary. Most rational people, however, are irrational about something, at least at sometime: politics, money, gambling, buying, eating, love, fear, hatred, and the like. Shakespeare capitalized on this characteristic with characters like Othello, who suffered fits of jealous rage, and Shylock, who hated all Christians. Solomon wrote astutely about the weaknesses of otherwise sane people. This includes the educated, the cognoscente, who often belie their training.

A definition of insanity is absurd or irrational behavior. Such behavior is so commonly reported that Aristotle's definition of man being a rational animal may be questioned. Mystics, soothsayers, healers, and miscreants have always been part of mankind. There is hope, however, in the fact most people deal daily with reality, to our benefit, and that through science we continuously gain better knowledge of the real world.

Sherman B. Nuland tells us that the great French physiologist and experimenter Claude Bernard (1813–1878) thought that man by nature is a metaphysical being who identifies feeling as reality and that experimentation does not come naturally to him (*The Mysteries Within*, 2000). Reason and science are hard-earned products of civilization which ignored leaves us at the mercy of anyone's opinion and only our feelings for reality.

CHAPTER 2

Genesis and Mathematics

ALEX HALEY'S STORY OF HIS AFRICAN ANCESTOR, KUNTA KINTA, WHO ARRIVED in North America as a slave in 1767, fascinated millions who read the book (published in 1976) and/or who watched the television series titled *Roots*. From the oral tradition presented to him by his grandmother, Haley traced his family history back seven generations, approximately one hundred forty years before his birth. Another notable figure, Benjamin Franklin, traced his ancestors back three generations with the help of oral tradition and gravestones. In 1757 Franklin set sail for England with two of his slaves, King and Peter, on a mission for the Philadelphia Assembly just ten years before Kunta Kinta arrived in the American Colony. Once in England, Franklin went to the ancestral town of his father at Ecton to collect oral family histories and visit the local graveyard, where Peter removed moss covering the gravestones. Franklin was delighted to learn, at age fifty-one, that he shared many of the characteristics of his uncle Thomas, then deceased (*The Private Franklin*, C.A. Lopez and E.W. Herbert, 1975). These genealogies start and end with the male, as is common, unless the female is a queen or some prominent person.

The genealogy of Jesus is long but differs in Matthew (1:1-17) and Luke (3:23-38). Matthew goes back to Abraham but Luke to Adam, and from David they are separate lines, touching Shealtiel and Zerubbabel (*Halley's Bible Handbook*, 1965). In any case, the text of Matthew is the most abbreviated and covers forty-two generations by name, with the total number from David to Jesus through Joseph being fourteen. Accepting that Mary was a virgin at the birth of Jesus, her genealogy to David would go back thirteen generations, representing

4

8,192 ancestors. Indeed, it is strange that Matthew and Luke traced the genealogy of Jesus through Joseph the carpenter.

The number of ancestors we have grows exponentially as $(2)^n$ where n represents the generation that proceeds us. Thus $(2)^1$ yields 2—our parents—while $(2)^2$ yields 4, our grandparents, as in the case of Franklin. In the case of Haley, who traced his origins back seven generations, the number of ancestors he had to that point is 128 or $(2)^7$. Each generation back obviously doubles the number of ancestors. When many generations are considered, the computation is facilitated by multiplying the log of 2 (0.301) by the generation considered and then taking the antilog of the product. Thus the antilog of 0.30103 (the log of 2) times 13 is 8,192. If one considers Mary's heredity back to the forty-one generations in the book of Matthew, the number of ancestors is astronomical: 2,199,000,000,000. This is of interest biologically and sociologically.

Molecular biologists recently completed the identification of the genes present in the human genome (*Science News*, vol. 159, February 17, 2001). In contrast to the 100,000 genes many thought previously, the human genome has about 30,000. Many of these genes are also present in bacteria, simple worms, and rats, among other living organisms. Indeed, the rat has the same number of genes. The human genome is large but many of the nucleotides are not genes. The difference between humans and rats depends upon how the genes orchestrate the formation of complex proteins. In any case, if we trace our ancestors back just fifteen generations, we find that there are more ancestors than genes (32,768). If we go back only seventeen generations, the number exceed 100,000 genes (131,072). Seventeen generations only represents 340 to 425 years, depending on whether 20 or 25 years is used to compute a generation. And one more generation would double this number to 262,144 individuals. It is apparent, therefore, that we are all remarkably related genetically and that only a few of these 30,000 genes separate one person from another. Many of us may lay claim to be related to William the Conquer, as does Charles, Prince of Wales, since the few genes that separated King William from others would be diluted in approximately fifty generations $(2)^{50}$.

That we share genetic pools is evident in the phenomenon of look-alikes. I have mistaken strangers at times for acquaintances and even old friends. Police records have revealed cases of false identity and twice I have been mistaken for another. Some years ago my wife and I took photographs of several sites in London and could not recall taking one photo of a building that appeared as though I was a

London pedestrian. Upon close examination it was another look-alike who was similarly dressed. It is said that Charlie Chaplin once entered a Chaplin look-alike contest in Italy and lost. It is also said that during World War II, look-alikes for Adolph Hitler and Winston Churchill were used for security reasons. On the other hand, only a few genes can greatly separate individuals, such as those for eye color or disease. Only one defective dominant gene causes the devastating affliction of Huntington's chorea that strikes either sex in middle age. Only chance determines whether the egg or sperm contains this one gene because the genetic material in these germ cells has been reduced to one-half of the adult. The defective gene that causes hemophilia occurred as a mutation in Queen Victoria and was devastating to ten male descendants of her royal family. By luck this gene did not affect the British. It was lost in the genetic shuffle between egg and sperm just as the unique genes that contributed to the characteristics of William the Conquer may be lost to that royal family. But some genes that gave rise to his liver, toenails, eye color, etcetera, must be common to mankind. Genealogy is more about names that genes. It is apparent that all of us have some genes common to Abraham, King David, the kings Ramses, Julius Caesar, or Milo of Croton if we go back far enough into our ancestry, whether starting with the survivors of Noah's ark or with Cro-Magnon man some 40,000 years ago.

CHAPTER 3

Genesis and Mankind

PALEOANTHROPOLOGISTS AND THE BIBLICAL ACCOUNT OF MAN'S BEGINNING
agree that early in our history there were few individuals. During the
reign of Queen Elizabeth I (1558-1603), about 3 million people
resided in the British Isles and now with Queen Elizabeth II, 65 million live there. The population of the earth has soared to some 6 billion since man's beginning. While this growth has been independent
of any one religion, it seems to have fulfilled the biblical directive to
be fruitful and multiply (Genesis 1:28, KJV).

It is unclear in the biblical account of man's beginning how many
humans were created on the sixth day of Creation. God apparently
consulted others in this creation for He said, "Let us make man in our
image," but upon making the final plans God created male and female
in His own image and instructed them to "be fruitful and multiply"
from this sixth day of Creation (Genesis 1:26–28, KJV). Biologically
this would require males and females to fulfill this command to multiply. He also provided food for His mankind and was pleased by the
end of the sixth day with what he had made (Genesis 1:31, KJV).
Indeed, He rested on the seventh day.

The creation of Adam, and later from one rib his wife Eve, in the
second chapter of Genesis is special and indicates he was made from
abundant materials of the earth prior to the appearance of rain
(Genesis 2:5). This may have occurred on the third day of creation
when grass, seed-bearing plants, and fruit trees appeared (Genesis
1:12). Biblically Adam may have been created just three days before
God made other male and female humans. These two accounts of
human Creation would explain why the elder son of Adam and Eve,
Cain, after killing his younger brother, was able to arrive in the land

of Nod, east of Eden, and obtain a wife (Genesis 4:16–17). Later Adam and Eve gave birth to another son, Seth. Both Cain and Seth fathered sons, Enoch and Enos, respectively. As written, Eve only had sons, so that the women created on the sixth day by God must have been her contemporaries. If not, her sons committed incest with siblings if Adam and Eve were the first and only product of God's human creation, and the writing indicates otherwise. In any case, the Bible, paleoanthropologists, and historians agree that at the beginning of mankind there were few humans compared to our present population.

Anthropologists have literally unearthed evidence that several groups of individuals who had many characteristics of modern humans lived prior to our arrival on earth but are now extinct. The most recent group to perish was the Neandertals (alternate spelling Neanderthals). They had a much larger brow ridge (bone above the eye socket or supra orbital ridge) than us and hardly any chin. Other skeletal differences are evident but because they buried their dead, managed fire, used crude tools, and bad a brain on average greater than present humans, they are considered a subspecies of modem man labeled *Homo sapiens neanderthalensis*. Moreover, his remains are found over wide areas of the old world: England, France, Germany, Italy, and Israel, among other sites. They apparently perished some 40,000 years ago.

A still older group had a very thick and straight brow ridge, no chin, and a keel top of the skull that is not like us. Their skulls were long but not nearly as high as ours. Their remains have been found in Africa, Europe, China, and even in the isle of Sumatra. Like us, they managed fire and made stone tools but are no longer with us, becoming extinct about one-half million years ago. Even though their teeth were similar to ours, anthropologists have named them Homo erectus.

Much older forms of life that walked erect like humans and used stone tools but had much smaller brains and much different facial features (prognathism, no chin, etc.) have been found by paleoanthropologists, named Homo habilis. These and other manlike creatures continue to be discovered. Anthropologists also tell us that we belong to a group of animals called primates because these all have fingernails and toenails, similar working thumbs (can touch each finger), and have four incisors. Moreover, since we have no tails, but do have crevices in our molars that are y-shaped, and carry our shoulder blades on the backside of the chest; we are further classified among the great primates referred to as apes. As one talented mechanic (FJ) once said to me "Those who don't believe we are related should visit a zoo." In any case, biologists have a right to label us as their data dictates. By even simple criteria we are animals, not plants.

While anthropologists and archeologists try to determine man's exact origin from a caldron of old dead bones and from our interrelationship with the family histories of other primates, there is an easy explanation as described by B.H. Edwards and in Genesis (chapters 6–9). Here, as many know, Noah was instructed to build an ark and gather, biologically speaking, animals from all over the world to be saved from a great flood. Most importantly he was to have his wife and his three sons and their wives on board (Genesis 6:18). After the great flood had killed all other living forms, humans included, the ark finally came to rest on the mountains of Ararat where eventually all departed (Genesis 8:15–16). The names of the three sons were Shem, Ham, and Japheth, and from these sons came all the nations of the earth (Genesis 9:18–19). More recently the theologian Edwards emphasized the importance of this biblical account by stating that, "These three sons were the start of the new world, and everybody today comes from them" (*Nothing but the Truth*, page 123, 1993). Therefore, the progeny of six individuals must have traveled extensively to reside in many different continents and become different enough in appearance to be termed the races of mankind.

Some descendents obviously went to Australia to become the Aborigine who were later nearly annihilated by their European kin. Some went to become the Japanese and the unique group of Ainu who over the centuries have been decimated by their Japanese kin. Others became the North American Indian (native American) who manifested conspicuous cheek (zygomatic) bones and unique incisors shaped in the back like a shovel. These inhabitants lost to their European relatives, as did the South American Indians. Although anthropologists reported differences in physical appearance of the American Indians, these people are, biblically speaking, all Noah's children. Other descendents migrated east to islands to settle as distinct-looking people of Melanesia, Polynesia, and others. Some went on land to become Indian, Tibetan, Chinese, Mongolian, Eskimo, and other peoples.

Those migrated south from Mount Ararat to continental Africa also became very diverse in appearance. Here some became the lean and extremely tall Nilotics (Dinka, Shilluk, etc.), Zulu, Bantu, Pigmy, Bushman, Ethiopian, Berber, and many other peoples. The tall Nuba near the heart of Africa today celebrate wrestling as did the ancient Greeks and Egyptians.

And we all know that those who traveled northward became nations of Slavs, Germans, and Nordics, who commonly have blond hair and blue eyes. Despite many centuries of war, rape, and mutual cohabitation, many so-called races still exist. There are no descriptions, photographs, or remains of Noah's immediate family to examine, but B.H. Edwards, among other theologians, assure us that from the genes of that one family sprang all forms of mankind in less than 4,000 years B.C.

CHAPTER 4

Genesis and Time

MANY OF THE IMMEDIATE DESCENDANTS OF ADAM AND EVE ARE LISTED IN THE Bible. The names of some of their sons and daughters are, however, unknown (Genesis 5:4) nor are the names of the males and females created on the sixth day known (Genesis 1:27), which would contribute to our genome. Nevertheless, Adam's son Seth was to His liking and his progeny is listed. They all lived a long time so that the modern definition of a generation apparently does not apply. From Genesis (5:5–32) we learn that Adam lived 930 years; Seth, 912; Enos (Enosh), 905; Cainan (Kenan), 910; Mahalalel, 895; Jared 962; Enoch, 365; Methuselah, 969; Lamech, 777; and Noah was 500 years old before he had three sons and lived 950 years. From this kind of information the Archbishop of Armagh, James Ussher, concluded in 1650 that the earth was created 4004 B.C. Later, Doctor John Lightfoot of Cambridge University, St. Catherine's College, refined this date to 9 o'clock A.M. October 23, 4004 B.C. (*Ancient Civilizations*, editor A. Cotterell, 1980).

One comforting aspect of religion is certainty. In contrast, thousands of astronomers, astrophysicists, geologists, paleobotanists, paleoanthropologists, and related scientists have spent billions of hours of study since 1830 to come to the conclusion that the earth started billions of years ago. Biblical teachers agree that nowhere do we have even an example of the original writings of the various authors named in the Bible, such as Moses, Isaiah, and Paul. But paleoanthropologists and biblical teachers must agree that no earthly human was an eyewitness to the early events that formed our earth. The former find that mankind appeared millions of years after the basic elements of the earth and after many creatures of land and sea were present. The

Bible clearly describes man's appearance on the sixth day of creation after the earth was formed and populated by plants and creatures of land and sea. Whoever is responsible for writing Genesis would agree with modern biologists that water is a prerequisite to life and states that water appeared on earth prior to living forms (Genesis 1:9-11). Edwards, among others, declares that all living forms and the Himalayan, Alpine, and all mountains were formed in six days and that Methuselah lived 969 years (*Nothing but the Truth*, B.H. Edwards, 1993). While there were no eyewitnesses to what transpired in the beginning, Edwards asserts that the times given in Genesis are correct but explains that mention of a rising or setting sun (Genesis 15:12, 17), which we all experience, was not intended to be a scientific description of celestial movements—only a common expression He does not explain how the sun and moon stood still until the Israelis killed their enemies (Joshua 10:13), nor why the sun moved backward ten degrees for Hezekiah (Isaiah 38:8). In either case, time would have been altered.

Edwards further agrees with Archbishop James Ussher that the year of creation was 4004 B.C. based on "the absolute reliability of biblical dates, even though the first book of Genesis was written thousands of years after Adam and Eve existed (*The Watchtower*, Vol. 120, No. 22, p.6, 1999). The *Encyclopedia Britannica* published in 1948, explains that the date 4004 B.C. put forth by James Ussher (1581–1656*)* as our beginning was derived from dates written on the margins of an early Bible by an unknown authority and that the Ussher biblical chronology has been disproved. Genealogists and biologists alike might also question these dates. Paleontologists and paleoanthropologists have amassed books of data and continue to find evidence of man's earlier appearance on earth. The textbooks of geology and astrophysics ignored the Ussher dating. Saint Peter provides some guidance concerning biblical time by reportedly stating, "one day is with the Lord as a thousand years and a thousand years as one day" (2 Peter 3:8, KJV). His statement makes us question the importance of insisting that the early verses of Genesis are scientifically accurate in time. Peter walked and talked with Jesus Christ, Ussher and Lightfoot did not.

For centuries it was held by most that the sun revolved around the earth based on the senses and because it was written in the Bible that the sun once stood still. The unsuccessful struggle that the great Italian physicist Galileo (Galileo Galilei, 1564–1642) had over planetary movements with theologians under Pope Paul V and with

Aristotelians is well documented. More recently Pope John Paul II declared that the church had erred in condemning Galileo as a heretic in 1633 and that the physical evidence of evolutionary change on earth over time is more than just a theory (CA 10/25/96). While professional geologists, archeologists, astrophysicists, paleoanthropologists, and others have spent years in disciplined training and years investigating prehistoric phenomena concerning the age of earth and man's arrival, no effort is required to ignore their findings. It is easy to read and still easier to be told about Genesis.

CHAPTER 5

Genesis and Zoology

SYNOPSIS: *NOAH AND HIS SMALL FAMILY WENT THROUGHOUT THE WORLD COLLECTING* *male and female of each animal species in a large ship as directed. The family gathered enough food for at least 57,000 living creatures and for themselves. During the Great Flood they did not touch land for five months and they kept 2,000 bats and 17,000 birds on board ship, kept the snakes from eating rats, and tigers from eating kangaroo. The family was undaunted by the stench and enormous quantity of excreta present during the voyage. Noah was a first-rate zoologist and taxonomist and the first to circumnavigate the earth without the help of sail or motor. His Herculean exploit has never been adequately told.*

Adam was directed to name every fowl and beast that was brought to him. This he did (Genesis 2:19–20). These names are not listed in the Bible but it must be granted that his descendant, Noah, had an extensive knowledge of zoology for he was told to collect male and female of fowl, cattle, and every creeping thing on earth prior to the Great Flood (Genesis 6:19–20). Botanical specimens were not mentioned, but he did as directed (Genesis 6:22, KJV). A modem biblical translation (TLB) more specifically states that he was to collect a pair of each kind of bird, animal, and reptile. The substitution of reptile for "every creeping thing" indicates that Noah need not be concerned with centipedes, worms, ants, spiders, and all creeping things. Although all three categories belong to the animal kingdom, the term *animal* is commonly a synonym for mammal, so that Noah was to collect all birds, mammals, and reptiles, male and female, present on earth. He was also told to gather special animals to be burnt later for religious ritual (Genesis 7:2; 8:20–21).

Noah was instructed to construct an ark (ship) 450 feet in length, 75 feet wide, and 45 feet high (in cubits: 300 by 50 by 30) to house the creatures he had gathered in anticipation of the Great Flood that was to destroy all other living forms (Genesis 6:17), including babies, children, women, and men, other than a few members of his immediate family (his wife, his three sons, and their wives).

The fact that Noah was told to bring the creatures to the ark (Genesis 6:19–20) was a Herculean task. He may have started east in India to collect poisonous reptiles like the king cobra, common cobra, banded krait, and the crocodylidae gavial (gharial). Also, the Indian rhinoceros, pigmy hog, honey badger (ratel), four-horned antelope, mountain weasel, sloth bear, red panda, Bengal fox, Rhesus macaque, bonnet macaque, gray mongoose, Indian palm squirrel, Kashmir pigmy, flying squirrel, Himalayan marmot, leopard cat, desert cat, snow leopard, Indian hare, Bengal tiger, and Indian elephant, to name a few. He would have caught many species of birds and went into the China highlands for giant pandas. He may have varied his route to collect the wild boar, yak, ibex, chamois, and wild ass.

He would have visited the islands of the southeast Asia to obtain pairs of the unique gibbon, orangutan (two species, one in Borneo and one in Sumatra), the proboscis monkey, the Java rhinoceros, the poisonous Fea's viper, and, of course, the komodo dragon.

He may have then gone to Australia and Tasmania for Johnston's crocodile, a king brown snake, a common death adder, a great gray kangaroo, the wallaby, a tree kangaroo, the fruit bat, the platypus, an echidna, a dingo, a Tasmanian devil, and wolf, pairs of emu, ostrich, and many other creatures.

Noah would have sojourned to Hawaii, Galapagos, and other islands to obtain various species of birds, mammals, and reptiles as he traversed the Pacific Ocean, but once he reached South and Central America, he would have found the neotropical rattlesnake, anaconda, barba amarilla, collared peccary, two-toed sloth, giant anteater, giant armadillo, common caiman, broad-snouted caiman, capuchin monkey, woolly monkey, spider monkey, howling monkey, water opossum, tapir, jaguar, and a plethora of magnificent birds. He would have also placed on his ark several llama, alpaca, and quanaco, and hundreds of species of bats. Zoologists must marvel at the ability of Noah to collect monkeys, including the monkey eagle and other creatures from the tree canopy of the great river Amazon. In this regard, Noah traveled to the remote northwest corner of the Amazon River to catch two monkeys (the Acari and Manicore marmosets) that only recently have been identified by zoologists (CA 4/23/00).

In North America he would have found specimens of the American alligator, Florida crocodile, water moccasin (cottonmouth), pigmy rattlesnake, diamondback rattlesnake, copperhead, coral snake, and many bats (leafchin,, leafnose, hognose, etc.). He would have collected many species of shrew (masked, long tail, etc.) and of moles (Townsend, hairytail, starnose, etc.). Larger animals would have been easier to find, including raccoon, beaver, coyote, pronghorn, Rocky Mountain goat, white-tailed deer, moose, elk, grizzly, black and Kodiak bears, bison, and mountain lion, wolverine, mink, red fox, gray fox, gray wolf, red wolf, river and sea otters, least weasel, bobcat, lynx, coati, woodchuck, badger, porcupine, mule deer, and white sheep, among others. His ark would have also housed many species of squirrel (red, flying, tassel-eared, etc.), mice (kangaroo, pocket, long-tailed, etc.), and many species of bird like the wild turkey, Cooper's hawk, robin, Carolina wren, and California condor. He also managed to collect all four species of skunk, male and female, found in North America.

When Noah went to the Arctic area to collect musk ox, caribou, arctic hare, arctic fox, and the polar bear, along with the snow owl and other creatures, is unknown. His travel to the Antarctic to collect various species of penguins (emperor, royal, king) would have been arduous.

At some time Noah must have obtained male and female poisonous snakes of Africa such as the spitting cobra, boomslang, black mamba, cape cobra, and other snakes. The Nile and African slender-snouted crocodiles are among other reptiles he would have collected. Camels (bactrian with two humps and Arabian with one hump) would have been added to his obligatory menagerie. Among other birds, he caught flamingo and the fish eagle and many mammals like the Savannah baboon, mandrill, Pate's monkey, kudu, brindle gru, Nubian giraffe, Grant's zebra, hippopotamus, black and white rhinoceros, warthog, lion, and African elephant. He must have been impressed with the differences between the mountain gorilla and the eastern and western lowland gorillas and between the common chimpanzee and the pigmy (bonobo) chimpanzee. Eventually he would have been delighted to note that the orangutans of Borneo and Sumatra differed from these other primates, unless he had such knowledge beforehand. After Africa he would most likely have visited Madagascar to obtain many unique species of that large island, especially lemurs, and later perhaps Europe for European hedgehog and European bison plus many more special birds, mammals, and reptiles.

Presumably Noah did not collect mammalian animals that live in or near the seas of the world because these may have been able to survive the Great Flood. If so, the number of elephant seal, baikal seal, bottle-nose dolphin, killer whale (orca), minke whale, humpback whale, sperm whale, manatees, and other like mammals would not have been decimated by the Flood. But changes in salinity and temperature of water would have been catastrophic for many aquatic forms of life. It is also unclear whether Noah had on board the American mastodon, which paleontologists tell us roamed North America for some 3 million years until about 10,000 years ago and was known to man. There were in addition three known species of mammoths (*primigenius, columbi,* and *jeffersonii,* named for the USA president Thomas Jefferson) on the mainland of the USA some years ago. The account of Noah's activity is too brief in Genesis to know whether he handled hundreds of dinosaurs, mammoths, the Irish elk, and other animals that are now extinct, but which creationists now claim co-existed with man (chapter 9 "Evil Evolution). His knowledge of bird migration must have been exemplary to collect such birds.

We do know that Noah had on board his ark food enough to feed the birds, animals, and reptiles for the duration of the Great Flood (Genesis 6:21). Noah was 600 years, two months, and seventeen days old when torrents of rain came down for forty days and nights (Genesis 7:11–12) until all high mountains were covered with water for 150 days (Genesis 7:20, 7:24). The water was twenty-two feet (fifteen cubits) and more above the highest peaks (Genesis 7:20, TLB, KJV). This means that the ark was floating higher than Mount Everest at nearly 30,000 feet (six and a half miles). Climatologists may be able to explain whether normal oxygenation could occur under these conditions for 150 days (five months) at that altitude, but the experience was most likely stressful for the 200 species of primates, 235 species of carnivores, 280 species of marsupials, nearly 1,000 species of bats, some 1,800 species of rodents, and thousands of species of birds, reptiles, and other animals. Indeed, there are today approximately 15,000 species of mammals (D. Hoffmeister: *Zoo Animals,* 1967), with male and female adding up to 30,000 of these animals, plus 8,500 pairs of birds (17,000 birds), and 5,000 different kinds of reptiles (10,000 reptiles) (*World Book Encyclopedia,* 1960). How much of the 450-foot-long ark was devoted to feed is unknown, but it must have been a challenge to keep at least 57,000 creatures alive with special diets for more than five months, not including the time taken to collect animals from all over the earth and the three months for the waters to subside after the ark rested on the 16,946 foot (3.2 miles) mountain of eastern Turkey called Ararat (Genesis 8:5, TLB). Eventually the birds, animals, and reptiles were released from the ship to go in pairs (Genesis

8:19). How the kangaroo, platypus, woodchuck, prairie dog, jaguar, Java rhinoceros, orangutan, mice, two-toed sloth, and others on the ark managed to return home is unknown.

There is archeological evidence that great local floods have occurred at different sites throughout the world (*Halley's Biblical Handbook*, H.H. Halley, 1965). The evangelical theologian B.H. Edwards discusses these local floods on page 288 of his text *Nothing but the Truth* (1993) and disproves the notion that the devastating flood described in Genesis was confined to the Middle East because the water rose six meters above the mountains, all life was destroyed, and he asks, "why was it necessary for him (Noah) to take on board representatives of all of the animals?" In other words, what was written in Genesis is proof that all mountains were covered with water and that 57,000 animals lived on the ark. Noah may have had some insects and "every creeping thing" on board the ark as mentioned in the King James Version (Genesis 8:17). In any case, it remains unknown how the great variety of plants and creeping animals not on board the ark spontaneously (*de novo*) sprang up all over our earth after the Great Flood had killed them.

By any criteria Noah was a remarkable person. He built a ship about half the length of the merchant vessel Queen Elizabeth (450 versus 1,031 feet). He went to the continents and islands of the world, and by water and land collected pairs of at least 28,500 species to take aboard his ark. He provided snails for the snail kite of Florida (this bird dies without snails for food), small fish for the dipper bird, bamboo for the giant panda, meat for the carnivores and great horned owl, and special diets for all 57,000 reptiles, birds, and mammals in his charge. He then fed and kept peaceful this menagerie for eight months on board from the start of the flood to the arrival of the ark on Mount Ararat. It is unlikely that any modern zoologist could do likewise.

Our Bible is not the first nor only to describe a great flood. The Babylonian one tells how King Xisuthros was told by a god to build a ship for his friends, all kinds of animals, and many provisions to ride out a flood. His ark landed on Mount Nisir in Armenia after the flood and he sent out a dove to see if it found other dry land. In Greece, Zeus became so disgusted with man that he tried to kill them all with a flood, like drowning rats. But the god Prometheus told his mortal son Deucalion to make a covered boat to house his wife Pyrrha and provisions to ride out a great flood. They landed on Mount Parnassus after the water subsided, appeased the gods, and the human race was reborn. *Halley's Bible Handbook* briefly describes eleven such traditional floods, from Egypt to Polynesia. The story in Genesis is attributed to Moses. He did not invent writing nor was he the first to tell of a great flood. His story is part of our religious tradition and experts tell us that great floods did occur in ancient times. In all great flood stories only a few survive to again populate the world. To ancient people of Mexico only one man, his wife, and children escaped; in Polynesia, eight survived; and so forth. All we know best is about the flood story Moses wrote, but if it is scientifically and historically without error, as the fundamentalists declare, then Noah and his family are the only ones to survive the only great flood and they must have done at least what is described herein. It is possible that Moses wrote Genesis for purposes other than for science and history.

CHAPTER 6

Cruel in His Image

ALTHOUGH PAUL WROTE THAT THE LOVE OF MONEY IS THE ROOT OF ALL EVIL (1 Timothy 6:10), a strong case can be made that cruelty plays that role in human behavior. Two versions of the Bible (TLB, RSV) repeat this admonition about loving money (Hebrews 13:5) while the KJV does not (Hebrews 13:5). In any case, it is cruel even to take advantage of others by lying to obtain money. Some murder to obtain money. The last five of the Ten Commandments deal with behavior toward our neighbors and these require an element of cruelty to break: must not murder, must not commit adultery, must not steal, must not lie, and must not covet your neighbor's possessions (Exodus 20:13–17). Indeed, covetousness caused King David to cruelly arrange to have Uriah die in battle so that he could freely cohabit with Uriah's wife, Bathsheba (2 Samuel 11:15).

Cruelty is most evident in our Old Testament, often occurring when God punishes for disobedience. After Eve ate the forbidden fruit, for instance, she was told that henceforth childbirth would be very painful while the desire to reproduce would persist (Genesis 3:16). This is a catch twenty-two situation. Queen Victoria of England accepted a solution when in 1857 she was administered chloroform to obtund the pain of parturition. This procedure was disconcerting to male preachers as it opposed God's scheme for women. The firstborn male of Adam and Eve, Cain, killed Abel (Genesis 4:8). When God was displeased with the wickedness of man, he produced the Great Flood that killed all babies, women, men, and all living forms except those saved on Noah's ark (Genesis 7:21; 8:16–19), as previously discussed. But this cleansing did not abolish the necessity for the cruel punishment of wickedness among Noah's descendents.

20

One descendent, Er, was so wicked that the Lord killed him (Genesis 38:7). The brother of Er, Onan, was instructed by his mother to marry his brother's widow Tamar and produce sons as the law required (Genesis 38:8). Onan resented this law because the sons produced were considered those of the dead Er. By practicing *coitus interruptus* Onan avoided impregnating Tamar and for this God killed Onan (Genesis 38:10). Tamar later deceived her father-in-law, Judah, into impregnating her, and before he discovered her true identity he was going to burn Tamar and the unborn child (Genesis 38:24). The law that resulted in the death of Onan is repeated in Deuteronomy (25:5–10) but countermanded in Leviticus (20:21). This difference was important during the reign of Henry VIII of England. He was married to Catherine, his brother's widow, in 1509 with the blessing of Pope Julius II under Deuteronomy but petitioned Pope Clements VII to dissolve the marriage in 1527 under Leviticus.

God told King Abimelech that he must return Sarah to her husband Abraham or he would be doomed to death along with all members of his household (Genesis 20:7), and later Abraham was directed to use a knife and sacrifice his only son, Isaac, to God. This turned out to be a cruel test of obedience (Genesis 22:1–12).

It is clear that if one fails to obey all of His commandments, He will punish by causing tuberculosis, fever, failed crops, wild animals killing children, parents eating their own children, and enslavement by enemies, among other acts of revenge (Leviticus 26:14–39, TLB). The Lord also demanded war to punish the Midianites where all of the males of Midian were killed, boys and women were killed, and God received booty for success. Only the little girls who had not been sexually active were spared (Numbers 31:1–41, TLB). God also instructed Joshua in detail how to destroy the city of Jericho and said all in Jericho had to be killed except the prostitute Rahab and her household members. Men, women, sheep, donkeys—everything was destroyed (Joshua 6:17–21, TLB). Then God sent Joshua to totally destroy the city of Ai and to kill everyone (Joshua 8:1–2; 8:25–26 TLB). Later God told Joshua not to fear the army assembled by the King of Jerusalem to fight the Israeli army (Joshua 10:8, TLB). He then caused panic so that Joshua could slaughter his enemies (Joshua 10:10). The Lord even stopped the sun as requested by Joshua to prolong daylight so that the slaughter of the army gathered by King Adoni-Zedek could continue to completion (Joshua 10:12–13, TLB). Joshua later attacked other cities (Makkedah, Libnah, etc.) and killed every last person (Joshua 10:28–30). This type of warfare today is termed ethnic cleansing and barbaric to many. But Joshua only did what the Lord commanded (Joshua 10:40).

Although "thou shall not murder" is one of the Ten Commandments of God (Exodus 20:13), under many situations killing and mutilating humans is demanded by the Lord. Thus in Exodus (TLB, KJV)) if a man accidentally kills a pregnant woman, he shall be executed (21:23); if a man's ox kills a human, the man shall be put to death (21:29); if a thief is killed at night while entering a home, the killer is not guilty (22:2); sorceresses (witches) shall be put to death (22:18); those guilty of bestiality must die (22:19); anyone who strikes a killing blow to another shall be put to death (21:12); anyone deliberately trying to kill another must be killed (21:14); men who commit adultery with another man's wife must die (Leviticus 20:10); and if a woman grabs the testicles of a man attacking her husband, she shall have her hand cut off without pity (Deuteronomy 25:11–12). And God puts to death those who do any work on the Sabbath (Exodus 31:15).

The young David knew he was doing God's work when he killed a giant uncircumcised Philistine by means of a stone to the forehead and death by sword, followed by decapitation (1 Samuel 17:49–51). David gave the carcass to animals to eat. During David's reign as king, God made the Israelis suffer three years of famine because one of them, Saul, had murdered the Gibeonites (2 Samuel 21:1). In anger at David, God sent the death angel and plague, which killed thousands and almost destroyed Jerusalem (2 Samuel 24:15–16).

Although God once threatened to compel parents to eat their children as punishment for wickedness (Leviticus 26:29), one mother actually resorted to cannibalism of her son with another mother to obtund the pangs of hunger. Both mothers agreed to eat each other's son on separate days. However, once hunger was satisfied, one mother hid her son so that neither could consume the remaining child. The mother of the dead boy revealed this deception to the king of Israel (2 Kings 6:26–30). Both the threat and the deed seem inordinately cruel. And every man worthy of death shall be executed for his own crime (Deuteronomy 24:16).

One of the great events of biblical times that is celebrated by millions today is the Passover. It is written that in one night God killed the firstborn son of every Egyptian and the firstborn male animal to persuade the Pharaoh of Egypt to free the Hebrews from slavery. The Israeli slaves were not affected that night because they had painted the lintel and sides of the doorway of their homes with the blood of killed lambs (Exodus 11:1–10, 12:1–13). The end of slavery was rightly celebrated but the Hebrews in turn had slaves who could share in the consumption of sacrificial food only if first they were painfully circumcised (Exodus 12:44). Today it seems inordinately cruel for God to have chosen to selectively kill young men and baby boys to terminate the slavery. Moses was also cruel in placing the value of sacrificial animals above the lives of innocent children when he and his followers were first offered their freedom by the Pharaoh (Exodus 10:24–25).

In the Old Testament God demands at times that animals be bled and burnt in His honor. Today this appears to be cruel, but details of the ritual was given to Moses which involved sprinkling blood upon the altar and burning the animals piece by piece, all according to the instruction of God (Leviticus 9:1–24). Earlier we learned that the smell of the burnt animal was pleasing to Him (Genesis 8:21 KJV). The ox, lamb, or goat must only be sacrificed at the tabernacle or otherwise whoever offers the sacrifice will be excommunicated from the nation and be guilty of murder (Leviticus 17:3–4 TLB). The Lord gave Moses detailed directions for declaring a person or a home to be free of leprosy that used bird blood, cedar wood, and other items (Leviticus 14:1–56), which today appear to be harsh.

Cruelty and murder is also evident in the New Testament. When Peter confronted two professed Christians, Annias and Sapphir, with cheating others of money, both died instantly (Acts 5:1–11). This illustrates that God is intolerant of dishonest Christians and not always loving as often stated by clerics. The death of Stephen, a disciple of Jesus, was presumably slower as he was stoned by a mob. Parenthetically, Benjamin Franklin aptly defined a mob as a monster with many heads but no brains. Our Lord was crucified by the Romans, their most severe and agonizing form of execution. Jesus was even flogged with a leaded whip beforehand (Mark 15:13). In those early times thousands were crucified in Assyria, Persia, and other countries. Alexander the Great reportedly had 2,000 inhabitants of Tyre crucified.

This inheritance of cruelty has been manifested throughout history. Thus the thousands of Christian children who followed the shepherd lad of France named Stephen in 1212 to free the Holy Land ended up as slaves in Egypt. Most of the boys and girls enslaved were under twelve years of age. When this children's crusade reached Marseilles, slave traders lured them to board their ships. The first Protestant Archbishop of Canterbury, Thomas Cranmer, served Henry VIII and King Edward VI well but was burned alive at the stake in 1556 under Roman Catholic Queen Mary. So one famous Christian roasted another famous Christian. While Henry VIII was still Roman Catholic and had earned the title in perpetuity of Defender of the Faith from Pope Leo X in 1521, he supported the burnings of Lutherans and like heretics, carried out by Sir Thomas More, Lord Chancellor of England. More also had a torture chamber in the basement of his home to deal with heresy. He was beheaded in 1535 even before King Henry was excommunicated by Pope Paul III in 1538. Around this time the Moslem Soleiman the Magnificent was killing Christians and occupied Buda and Pesth, Hungary, in 1529. Martin Luther died in 1546 and German Lutherans and German Catholics began killing each other (H.G. Wells, *Outline of History*, 1940). Eventually different countries became involved in this religious war and in 1618 the Thirty Year's War officially started. More recently Hindu conservatives of India have attacked Christians and Moslems and burned the current Pope in effigy (CA 11/6/99). Violence between Moslems and Christians occurs in Nigeria (CA 12/15/99) and 2,000 have died recently in Indonesia during Moslem-Christian clashes despite appeals by moderate Islamic leaders for an end to holy wars against Christians (CA 1/20/00). But there is hope. In 1999 the Lutheran Bishop Krause and Pope John Paul II met in Augsbury, Germany, and embraced. This seems to end 500 years of animosity between two major faiths (CA 11/1/99).

Cruelty is independent of age and gender. Women murder, even their own children. One mother drowned her three-year-old and fourteen-month-old sons by rolling her car into a lake with the boys strapped in seat belts. She diverted attention from herself by claiming a carjacker had taken the boys inadvertently. She pleaded for the return of her sons (CA 6/20/96). Another mother stabbed to death her five and six-year-old sons and appealed for help to find the human animal responsible for their murder (CA 6/20/96). In England a nurse murdered children on her hospital ward (CA 5129/93), in Minneapolis a young teenage mother placed her newborn in the garbage (CA 1/13/00), in Delaware a boy and girl left their newborn to die in a trash bin (CA 11/21/96), and one female naval cadet helped her fiancé murder a girl by smashing her skull with a barbell weight (CA 9/8/96). And a mother and her daughter schemed successfully to have the head of John the Baptist delivered on a tray, which the daughter carried to her mother (Matthew 14:11, KJV).

Two girls and two boys made plans to murder their fifth grade teacher by poison in Virginia (CA 8/24/97) and two young brothers in

Detroit almost killed by torture a three-year-old girl left in their charge (CA 6/11/99). Near my home three teenagers brutally murdered a sixty-three-year-old woman after carjacking her automobile (CA 6/17/99). *The Commercial Appeal* (3/25/98) nicely summarized the murder of children in schools in Tennessee and three contiguous states by other children fourteen to seventeen years of age. Thirty-seven people were shot in four schools and thirteen died. One teen also killed his mother by cutting her throat and another opened fire at students holding a prayer meeting. Mass murders by teenagers for a while seemed to be regional events until the violence at Columbine High School, Colorado.

Six young girls told parents and police that a fifty-two-year-old man had given them Halloween apples that contained concealed razor blades. The judge in charge would have whipped the man if lawful, and the neighbors wanted to burn the guy's home. Later several of the girls confessed that the story was a lie and the accused man was released from jail (CA 11/5/69). One fourteen-year-old girl in Tennessee planted a bomb hoping to destroy her school and kill the principal (CA 3/19/00), and three teenage boys whose ages ranged from fourteen to sixteen bludgeoned to death a teacher in Denver, Colorado (CA 1/13/00). In Arkansas two teenage boys were arrested for beating to death a high school classmate who was pregnant (CA 2/8/00). In Memphis a teenager planned to bomb a home and with the help of others shoot the occupants as they ran from the explosion (CA 4/15/00). And cruel hazing continues to be a problem among college fraternities. One student recently died after being required to ingest an excess amount of alcohol (CA 3/26/00) and five fraternity recruits were hospitalized after being severely beaten (CA 5/17/98).

Cruelty also seems to be a sport for some. One university student was killed and others shot at while fishing. It was labeled a random act of murder (CA 6/11/99). One serial killer videotaped his victims begging for their lives before being tortured and murdered in California. Six men, three women, and even two baby boys were killed by this one person (CA 7/1/99). In Belgium one man killed and dismembered six women (CA 4/26/97). One man obsessed with guns and the Bible killed three and wounded five other humans before he was arrested for shooting his teenage sister in the back. His goal was to kill one person for each of the twelve Zodiac signs (CA 6/20/96). In Ireland one political leader and his son were shot while attending services in a Roman Catholic Church (CA 5/17/98), and the mayor and city council members were fired upon at City Hall, Riverside, California, by a disgruntled former employee (CA 10/7/98). Apparently for revenge, one male in Oregon who was evicted from a private party of 200 returned and fired a gun into the group (CA 1/4/99). In the Philippines someone lobbed a grenade at a large crowd who were watching firemen fight a blaze. Ten spectators were killed and seventy-four injured from the explosion (CA 1/4/99). One fifteen-year-old girl was raped in 1978 and then the rapist chopped off her forearms, but she lived. The rapist was released after eight years in prison and afterward stabbed to death a prostitute (CA 3/9/97). At one time the pirates of Malaysia would take the cargo from captured ships, but more recently they kill the crew and take all (CA 2/3/99).

The Bible also reminds us that some women are cruel, perhaps by nature. Delilah was one who nagged Samson, who loved her dearly, to reveal that his dead hair was the source of his great strength (Judges 16:4–31). She was paid well for this information by the Philistines who then chained him and gouged out his eyes. Jezebel was queen as the wife of Ahab king of Israel, who tried to kill all prophets of Jehovah (1 Kings 18:4 and 13), but the prophet Elijah hid one hundred from her. Even though God had once sent ravens to feed Elijah (1 Kings 17:4) and gave him the power to restore life to a boy (1 Kings 17:23) and helped him kill all the prophets of Baal (1 Kings 18:40), when the evil queen swore to kill him, Elijah fled for his life (1 Kings 19:3). Perhaps the most sinister was Herodias who, with the help of her daughter Salome, managed to have the head of the righteous John the Baptist delivered on a platter (Matthew 14:1–12), 2), as previously mentioned.

One famous act of cruelty was committed in Chicago in 1924 by two brilliant young college graduates, Richard Loeb and Nathan Leopold. Loeb was the youngest graduate of the University of Michigan and Leopold at fourteen had graduated from the University of Chicago. They kidnapped and murdered a fourteen-year-old neighbor, Robbie Franks, for the thrill of committing the perfect crime (*The People's Almanac*, #2, by D. Wallechinsky and I. Wallace, 1978). As a boy I remember adults discussing this dastardly, senseless crime. They did not murder for money, only for fun. Neither showed any remorse for their misadventure.

The love of money cannot account for most of the evil committed. Was the Holocaust carried out by thousands because of this singular love? How much money was gained by the rebels of Sierra Leone who amputated both forearms of infants in the year 2000? The atrocities committed recently by gangs, tribes, and religious or ethnic groups in Somalia, Sudan, Jerusalem, Yugoslavia, Ireland, and else-where appear unrelated to the love of money. The photographer and writer Robert Caputo describes in *Journey Up the Nile* (1988) much of the beauty and brutality that is Africa today. In Uganda he gave a ride to a policeman who was witness to the terrorism under Idi Amin and the later President Milton Obote of Uganda, once a prosperous coun-try. The policeman summarized perfectly the problems created by cruelty: "We could grow anything here," he said. "We could be rich, but we cannot find peace."

Most people wish to be wanted or needed, at least by someone: parents, friends, teammates, church members, spouses, fellow work-ers, and employers. This is one aspect of another common desire, to influence others as parents, teachers, politicians, preachers, co-work-ers, academic deans, and so forth. When these desires are not fulfilled there is the feeling of estrangement, resentment, rejection, and/or loneliness. But those who are wanted, needed, and have influence feel important. Those who influence many are said to be powerful. When cruelty is added to this mix, every type of behavior is manifested, from bullying and child abuse to sadistic gang members and the Hitlers of this world.

Perhaps everyone has been cruel at sometime in their life: teasing, lying about others, and throwing stones at the innocent. I remember students breaking school windows and indiscriminately slashing bicy-cle tires of other students. Children are notoriously cruel to the unusual child and often to siblings. A few have murdered for no apparent reason. Studies indicate that demeanor is largely determined by heredity. Identical twins reared apart have remarkably similar per-sonalities, interests, and even vocations. Nevertheless, with good par-ents, good schools, good communities, and/or good luck, millions ultimately achieve civility. While there are many honest, good-natured people, evil is so pervasive that we teach children to avoid friendly strangers and feel at risk when strangers seek a ride or profess a need to enter our home. Walter Hess was awarded the Nobel Prize in 1949 for demonstrating that electrical stimulation of different parts of the brain produced different behaviors that ranged from rage to peaceful sleep. Others have shown that rage attacks in animals and humans can be stopped by electrical stimulation. Such studies have identified pleasure (reward) centers and areas of the brain that evoke vivid memories of past events, among other phenomena. These experiments seemed to be mapping the mind but have not explained why cruelty is a source of pleasure. A larger question is why people who profess godliness may become so perverse in their belief that they abandon humanity and murder children and others who they deem unworthy of God's blessing.

Making someone, anyone, uncomfortable for no obvious reason suggests that cruelty is one inherent motive of human behavior. Why else do the vandal, the bully, the pugnacious, the sadistic, the acrimonious, and the ruthless derive satisfaction from such behavior? The Bible is replete with stories—starting with the murder of Abel by his brother Cain—where cruelty is central to the event. Without cruelty thoughts of murder, revenge, robbery, rape, and the like would be impotent. We were made in His image, we are taught, and the Bible states we naturally love to do evil things (Galatians 5:17, TLB) and by nature we are children of wrath (Ephesians 2:3, RSV). While love of money may be an evil, Ecclesiastes tells us that "money gives everything"(10:19, TLB) or "money answereth all things" (10:19, KJV). Paul seems to have been mistaken or misquoted.

CHAPTER 7

Kant Said It All

IMMANUEL KANT (1724–1804) WAS A CHILD OF POOR PARENTS AND AS A BOY was taught by dogmatic, harsh Pietists. One of his teachers stated that he would rather save one soul than produce a hundred scholars (*Living Biographies of Great Philosophers*, H. Thomas, D.L. Thomas, 1941). Nevertheless, he grew to revel in the intellectual freedom of enquiry afforded by mathematics and physics and later turned his attention to metaphysics. Although his philosophical writings were ponderous, he was beloved as a teacher and by the citizens of Konigsberg, then part of Prussia. As a philosopher he examined (critiqued) the mentation involved in pure reason, practical reason, and judgment. In so doing, he seems to have touched upon every argument for and against religion.

In his analysis of pure reason, Kant concludes that we cannot prove the existence of God because of the limitations of our senses. To many this would seem self-evident. Our understanding of the real world depends on these imperfect sensory experiences and the way our brain reacts or interprets the experience. Without the brain the eye is impotent but, as Kant might argue, what we see is intellectual. To many any snake is just a snake, but an expert sees more. The world's largest gorilla, Bushman, who lived many years at the Lincoln Zoo in Chicago, was fearful of a garter snake. I have known humans who reacted similarly but by training the herpetologist reacts realistically. So says Kant, our knowledge of the real world depends on concepts as well as on perceptions. However, since our concepts and ideas are imperfect and our senses are limited, we cannot be too certain, he says, about anything (maybe death and taxes). In any case, the agnostic would agree that the existence of God can neither be proved nor disproved. The atheists and biblical inerrant dogmatists have their own concept of certainty.

Kant tells a different story in his examination of practical reason. He argues that if religion cannot be based on science, it can fulfill a practical need in our lives based on morals or rectitude. It is not a matter of pure reason but of practical reason. We believe in God because we need such a belief, he says. In this regard, I embrace religion for many earthly reasons. It provides a camaraderie and peace of mind that is appealing. It can comfort those who have lost loved ones and add beauty to marriages. I love the concept of heaven and to hear little children sing in church. A good homily by clergymen is pleasing to many and gives new significance to the text, content, and message of Jesus. Many other church functions are pleasant and religious instruction has enhanced civility among millions of children and adults. Prayer has alleviated anxiety and clarified problems. Why any of us need to believe in the supernatural is a mystery, but social anthropologists and archeologists report that all social groups have embraced some form of divine worship. A recent survey indicates that 40 percent of scientists do pray, that 45 percent hold some concept of God, and that about 15 percent have no definite belief (CA 4/3/97). Benjamin Franklin, George Washington, and Isaac Newton are great men of history who held a firm belief in God. Yet there is no evidence that their religious beliefs per se prevented them from facing reality or caused irrational behavior. On the other hand, thirteen people were nailed to crosses recently to celebrate Easter in the Philippines (CA 4/22/00) and thirty-nine members of Heaven's Gate were inspired by Marshal Applewhite to commit suicide in California, with the help of modern science (alcohol, pentobarbital, and asphyxiation), to catch a ride on an imagined rocket that followed the Hale-Bopp Comet (CA 3/28/97). Charles E. Dull (*Modern Chemistry*, 1942) wrote that J.O. Frank recorded 1,800 different things about which some citizens of the USA are superstitious, like carrying lucky pieces. Followers of David Koresh chose to die with him in Waco, Texas, in 1993 because he was God in flesh (CA 6/20/00). When the older brother of Horace Mann drowned in 1810 while swimming on Sunday, the Calvinist preacher, Dr. Emmons, declared that the boy most probably is in Hell (*Horace Mann*, by J. Treichler, 1962). While his sobbing mother accepted this as God's judgment, Mann later worshiped with a different Christian denomination. Why faith, like Proteus, takes so many different forms is imponderable. With horoscopes everywhere and new age psychics, many people even draw on the supernatural independent of God. In any case, Kant argues correctly that for practical reasons we, at least most of us, believe in the unproved to fulfill an intuitive need.

Lastly, Kant in his *Critique of Judgment* judges that nature may be the best evidence of God. While God remains a riddle that may never be solved, he says, every painting presupposes an artist and our universe presupposes a Creator. In 1802, just two years before Kant died, William Paley argued that every design has a designer and presented his often cited story that upon finding a watch we know there was a watchmaker. Psalm 19 presents the idea directly in asserting that the firmament (sky and space) shows His handiwork. G.L. Shroeder in his book *The Science of God* (1997) devotes a chapter to the watchmaker theme. He points out that living things are not created like watches and, without rejecting the watchmaker idea, goes on to discuss mathematical probabilities concerning mutation rates and some molecular biology involved in evolution. Many seem to accept and foster the notion that nature is the handiwork of God. I have heard successful surgeons tell patients that they only did the surgery while God did the rest. Some say nature healed. Sherlock Holmes commented at the conclusion of one mystery ("The Navel Treaty") that "Our highest assurance of the goodness of Providence seems to me to rest in the flowers." The Italian entomologist Adriiano Zanetli, however, reminds us that the colors and scents of flowers were made for insects. Perhaps the scents of man were made for mosquitoes. In a cartoon by Bil Keane, one little boy remarks that God did a pretty good job creating "but he sure messed up with flies" (CA 8/21/02). There is not much religious celebration when surgery fails or when missionaries and others die from amebiasis, trypanosomiasis, or suffer from head lice (Pediculus). When adults suffer and die from hereditary disease like Huntington's chorea, babies are born with horrendous birth defects such as ancephaly, when thousands die from hookworm infestation or malaria, there seems to be little praise for any great design by the watchmaker. Considering the billions (and billions) of people who have lived and do live on earth; it is remarkable that only a handful of scientists have identified causes, found treatments for, and even eradicated some of the many diseases of mankind. In the Middle Ages astrologers attributed the Black Death (caused by the bite of fleas carrying the bacterium *Yersinia pestis* that the fleas got from rats) to the poor alignment of Saturn, Jupiter, and Mars (*A History of Medicine*, by L.N. Magner, 1992). In 1348 Pope Clement VI went from his court in Avignon to Rome to abolish this plague, to no avail. The pestilence was more powerful. Even today we hear of fabulous cures of medical conditions that occur at shrines, holy wells, and in front of preachers. In *The Pleasure of Finding Things Out* (1999), Richard Feynman suggests that such holy cures be investigated scientifically to ascertain whether the rate or number of cures can be improved. Instead of a cure here or there, thousands of people suffering from leukemia, diabetes, blindness, hepatitis C, parkinsonism, epilepsy, herniated spinal discs, encephalitis, stroke, dislocations, Alzheimer's, kidney failure, heart failure, hemophilia, influenza, and countless afflictions might benefit from such a study. Holy intervention and prayer has not stopped bubonic plague, yellow fever, or malaria. However, a caring attitude toward the ill and good nursing care promotes healing, which the ancient Greek physicians used to good advantage. Prayer can instill hope and relieve anxiety but does not empty the garbage. Part of the riddle Kant dealt with was that both good and bad seems to be inherent in nature or God.

A more recent argument that some use in support of the watchmaker concept is based on findings during the past forty years in the field of molecular biology. The essence of the argument is that the function of cells, as revealed by scientists, is so complex that God must have started it all. Prior to 1960 much emphasis was placed on the 1,000- plus roles proteins play in biological functions—in energy production, muscle contractions, formation of neurotransmitters, digestion, blood coagulation, immunity, etc. In 1953 Stanley L. Miller published a remarkable result, showing that all of the building blocks of proteins (amino acids) could be produced from the gases methane (CH_3), hydrogen, ammonia (NH_3), and water vapor in the presence of electricity (*Science*, Vol. 117, p.528). The manufacture of these essential amino acids under such primitive conditions from gases prompted one well-known atheistic British scientist to remark that now he could die in peace. By adding another gas, carbon dioxide, to the mix scientists have now produced sugars, purines, and pyrimidines, which are constituents of the nucleolides of DNA, when the gaseous mix is activated by electricity or ultraviolet light. Texts on molecular biology state that it is surprising how easy it is to produce these organic compounds that are so basic to life. Other organic compounds, like urea, that are products of living organisms also emerge from the gaseous mix. While biochemists commonly relate how these fundamental compounds could be involved in the evolutionary phenomenon, the scientific creationists point out that these organic compounds are not living organism and that no one knows the exact physical conditions at the beginning of life. They conclude, without experimentation, that we do not need to abandon morals for evolution because life is too complex.

The complexity creationists like to talk the most about is DNA, the mother substance of our genes, which sends chemical signals from the nucleus of cells which combine with amino acids in such a way as to cause the formation of proteins. The proteins in turn make the nucleotides that are used to form new DNA when the cell divides to make two new complete cells (replication). So it resembles the chicken and egg riddle: Did the proteins or DNA (genes) come first? With the help of some minerals and vitamins (which proteins make in plants), the proteins do the work of the cell, like the worker bees doing all the work to maintain the queen and her eggs. Many proteins bind to the well-known double helix structure of DNA (gene regulatory proteins, zinc finger proteins, etc.) and are essential for gene activity. Some proteins unzip the DNA double helix (topoisomerases), others zip up the helix (polymerases), and others tie the ends of the helix (teleomerases) to define the chromosomes.

When chromosomes divide they are drawn to opposite sides of the cell by proteins called microtubules and eventually two new cells are constructed by proteins. The membrane of our cells contain thousands of different receptor proteins (glycoproteins) for insulin and countless substances, and the skeleton of cells are made of proteins (more microtubules). Proteins destroy potentially harmful compounds of oxygen, acting as antioxidants (hydrogen peroxidase, glutathione peroxidase), and are essential for the digestion of food, muscle contractions, and nerve conduction, among thousands of other functions. In turn the DNA responds to the needs of our bodies by making more proteins and even orchestrates the destruction of damaged cells (apoptosis) by producing special proteins (P53, etc.) to make way for repair. I embrace the idea that God started it all, but there is no science in the proclamation of some that the complexity of life is proof of God. The complex life cycle of parasites and countless deadly diseases, new and old, is hardly proof that a moral, benevolent watchmaker started it all. The beginning of it all may turn out to be simple. Nevertheless, Kant would probably agree that there is no harm in the personal belief that what man did not start, God did.

CHAPTER 8

The Nature of Science

THE MAN WHO TAUGHT CHEMISTRY AND PHYSICS AT THE HIGH SCHOOL I ATTENDED also introduced to his students the practical aspects of the scientific method. Mr. Apostle (his real name) came to America from Greece as a teenager. Everything he taught appeared to have practical applications, even though student grades were based on standardized examinations from California. It was general knowledge that Mr. Apostle, as a widower, reared successfully two splendid daughters and that he regularly worshipped at the Congregational church. After demonstrating some principle of physics or chemistry, he often passed around his hat to collect pennies, paper clips, hairpins, or some trivia as his reward. Occasionally, he would offer a dollar to any student who could answer a difficult question. In those days a dollar was worth four adult admissions to the movies and ten to twenty standard candy bars. Despite such antics, his demeanor won respect even from the tough guys in school. Although Mr. Amedei ably taught biology, Mr. Apostle was conversant in that area of science and occasionally reminded us of the wonders of Mother Nature. He told of some of his experiences in biology as a student at Indiana University. Once he inadvertently saw his botany professor praying early in the morning while on a field trip. By any criteria he was a splendid person and science teacher.

Many articles dealing with the nature of science differ in content and presumably reflect, in part, the author's experience. However, I have found the discussion by Mr. Apostle most practical and not too unlike that written by Abraham Wolf in 1928 (A. Wolf, *Essentials of Scientific Method*) or presented in the 1960 issue of *World Book Encyclopedia*. With some embellishment, the following is what Mr.

Apostle taught concerning the nature of science. Mr. Apostle wrote the following on the blackboard to enable us to better follow the topic:

    A. Formal sciences
        1. Mathematics
        2. Logic
    B. Empirical sciences
        1. Observation
        2. Experimentation
    C. Inductive and Deductive Reasoning

The formal sciences are mathematics and logic. Apparently these are formal because of the strict rules that govern their applications. Mathematics has been classified as applied and pure. The pure may have no practical application, like having lines extend to infinity or proving Fermat's theorem. However, what begins as pure mathematics often becomes useful. For instance, statistical tests were rarely used in biology prior to 1940, but they are now routinely applied to help evaluate the efficacy of drug therapies and many experimental results. The golden mean of Fibonacci (circa A.D. 1202) is so evident in nature, from seashells to galaxies, that some have said that God is a mathematician. The combination of mathematics with logic by George Boole (1815–1864), called symbolic logic or mathematical logic, has been essential to the computer industry. E.T. Bell describes the remarkable achievements and diverse personalities of this group of scientists in *Men of Mathematics* (Simon and Schuster, NY, 1937). The chapter on Carl Friederich Gauss (1777–1854) who rose from rags to become among the three greatest mathematicians is priceless. As a formal science, mathematics needs in essence only pencil and paper for its execution. The same may be said of the rules of logic. The other branches of science require more, but all use different aspects of the formal sciences to organize data, strengthen conclusions, and even predict events in the real world. The popular physicist and Nobel laureate, Richard Feynman, said of the role mathematics plays in science, "It just turns out that you can state mathematical laws, at least in physics, which work to make powerful predictions." He further said, "Why nature is mathematical is, again, a mystery" (*The Meaning of It All*, p.24, 1998).

Observation and experimentation are the keystones of the empirical sciences. With observation, at least in theory, the objects or behavior studied are not modified by the scientist. The migration of birds, weather patterns, astronomy, geology, paleontology, and anatomy are examples of observational sciences. A key component of the observational sciences is descriptive. Much of medicine is descriptive of symptoms and signs. James Parkinson (1755–1824), for instance, described one neurological affliction so vividly that the condition is called Parkinson's Disease. Naturalists, botanists, entomologist, and marine biologists draw, photograph, and describe to classify new species they may find. Jane Goodall observed for years the behavior of wild chimpanzees in Africa to become a celebrated scientist. Microscopes, binoculars, telescopes, radiometers, and other devices may be used to collect data by the observer. Chemical analysis of structures seen under the microscope may be performed to reveal the composition of the object. From the data observers can draw conclusions and make generalizations such as birds have feathers and lay eggs or that there is less oxygen at higher than at lower elevations. Statements like mammalian red blood cells are red because of the presence of oxyhemogloblin and leaves are green because of chlorophyll are conclusions we accept as true. The plethora of new observations is the result of advances in technology. Initially few research institutes could afford electron microscopes but by 1960 these were common and greatly multiplied observations. The result has been descriptions of viruses and many minute structures never before seen. The telescopes and other sensors sent into space have likewise brought remarkable new data. One of my mentors, Harold Himwich, M.D., used to say that new methods make new science. X-ray established radiology and the microscope histology, for instance. With observation, what you see is what you get. If you determine the amount of lead in water, what you find is what you get. By chemical analysis objects can be classified as mineral, protein, carbohydrate, etc. The task of the taxonomist is to classify living things. The facts obtained may simply remain facts or observers may propose a theory to explain why their observations are scientifically important.

Experimentation is the other keystone of the empirical sciences. The essence of experimentation is control over the phenomena studied. The term *experiment*, however, is often correctly used in observational science because of the use of instrumentation or chemicals but this may lead to confusion. Students may use iodine in an experiment, for instance, to detect starch in foods or do an experiment with a calorimeter to determine the energy substances may yield when oxidized. The mere use of technology is not, however, experimentation unless there is a control over the phenomenon observed. With experimentation the activity of natural phenomena is modified to reveal how things work and how nature might work for us. Controlled experiments may result in laws such as Ohm's Law in electricity or Charles's Law of gases. Thomas A. Edison (1847–1931) manipulated materials to create electric lighting and other remarkable inventions. He had a practical knowledge of the materials used that he applied largely by trial and error to achieve greatness. His comment concerning his success was that genius is one percent inspiration and ninety-nine percent perspiration. Albert A. Michelson (1852–1931) created experiments that measured the speed of light in vacuum, air, water, and glass, finding the vacuum yielded the fastest reading of 186,310 miles per second. In the biological sciences, including medicine, experimentation often matches a control group with an experimental group. Often only one factor separates the groups. For instance, the only factor that separates one group of plants from another may be the amount of potassium in the soil, or it might be the amount of light exposure, to see if the experimental group responds better or worse than the control. One group of patients may be given a new drug and another (control) group a placebo for comparison. Sometimes the new drug is compared with one that has been used for years. One group of rats with similar heredity may be given special diets or drugs to see if learning or longevity differs from their close relatives. An example of biological experimentation conducted without group comparison was performed by Otto Loewi (1873–1961), who was awarded the Nobel Prize in 1936. Loewi electrically stimulated nerves that ended in the hearts of frogs and ultimately showed that nerve stimulation caused the heart to slow because the nerve released a substance called acetylcholine. Others confirmed this finding and it became a fact that nerves release chemicals that change heart function.

The difference between observation and experimentation in science often seems obscure and unimportant. For instance, Hans Berger used the instrument developed by Einthoven, which recorded from outside the skin the electrical discharges from the beating heart, to see if electrical activity from the brain could also be recorded from the skin covering the cranium. He observed that the brain did produce its own electrical activity, as an electroencephalogram (EEG). He then did experimentation to show that the EEG changed with repose, mental activity, and light. Within limits, Berger could control the pattern of the EEG with the cooperation of the subject. Later the EEG was useful to classify types of epilepsy, help detect brain tumors, and detect sleep abnormalities. The distinction between observation and experimentation seems hazy at times, but this old classification of scientific methodology remains practical. In general, with observation objects and subjects are described, identified, and classified. With experimentation objects and subjects are manipulated (controlled) to create new chemical compounds and discover factors that govern physical and biological phenomenon.

Mentation called inductive logic is common and paramount to most scientific studies. By induction a hypothesis is proposed to explain the facts discovered by investigators. As Bertrand A. Russell (1872–1970) said, "Science starts, not from large assumptions, but from particular facts discovered by observation or experimentation" (*Religion and Science*, Oxford University Press, 1935). Russell then points out that the findings may lead to a working (tentative) hypothesis. If new facts support the hypothesis, a theory is formed. A new hypothesis or theory can emerge if new facts do not support the original one. Thomas S. Kuhn wrote a book concerning the turmoil and conflict often associated with changing a strong theory, usually in physics (*The Structure of Scientific Revolutions*, University of Chicago Press, 1996). Kuhn uses different terminology than Russell or Mr. Apostle to describe inductive logic starting with normal science (facts) to hypothesis and then to paradigm (theory). As scientific procedures continue to be more sophisticated, many theories have been modified over the years. Russell refers to the steps taken to form and modify theory as Science's Method. In any case, the conclusions, inferences, and theories in science are based on the best facts available. Junk science is based on faulty experiments or observations that do not endure. But one theory may be modified or replaced as the findings warrant. The great value of theory is that it offers an explanation of the phenomenon studied and, as important, it can suggest new studies. When a new study is based on theory (or hypothesis), the intellectual process is termed deduction, which is commonly a prediction of what should happen with experimentation or what may be found through observation if the theory is correct. The new study derived from deduction (prediction) may turn up facts that support or may modify the theory into a new one. Thus the induction process can lead to a deduction that upon experimentation or observation yield new data that may or may not support a hypothesis. While scientific logic may be of interest mostly to philosophers, it is simple enough to be grasp by young students as taught by Mr. Apostle. And the concepts may have lasting argumentative value. When individuals proclaim their theory, as gurus often do, we should ask more about the facts. When some proclaim dogmatically that a theory is only a theory, not a fact, we should ask what facts are being dismissed.

One chapter in the aforementioned book by Feynman deals with the uncertainty of science. Here he emphasizes that science is based on the best information available, not authority, but that conclusions concerning natural phenomena do change with new and better observations. This is more obvious to those who do research than to students who learn of the exactitude of science. The laws of Avogado, Boyle, and Gay-Lussae in chemistry have stood the test of time with certainty. If the house is wired correctly, the lights will go on. In most areas of science, technology, and engineering there is little room for maybe and uncertainty. Feynman extols the value of objectivity in science that he declares is the principle of observation as judge and was informing students that there are many questions about the universe (uncertainties) to explore. Also, since science is based on the best evidence available, objectivity does not guarantee certainty. The number of elements found in a rock, for instance, may increase with newer methods, and concluding that a particular fish is extinct may be false. He also stated that each generation should be taught what is commonly referred to as the scientific method. Other academicians echo this concern, complaining that modern high school authors "don't seem to understand what science is about" (CA 1/15/01) and that recent Ph.D. graduates are ignorant of scientific reasoning and are experts instead of scholars (CA 4/7/02). Apparently there is a need to teach each generation what science is about. This Mr. Apostle tried to do, but many of the younger generation are not taught as the following two stories attest. Carl Baugh in a book published 1999 stated that, "evolution is not empirical" (that is, it can not be proven with rigid and unbiased scientific procedures). He abhors the theory of evolution and is ignorant of the meaning of empirical findings. He should have consulted a *Webster* dictionary or the *World Book Encyclopedia* to avoid this mistake. Also, one young faculty member (PB) I knew was enamored with obtaining grants from the National Institutes of Health (NIH) which required statements concerning aims, goals, and working hypothesis to win funding. This sounds sophisticated, but these items were originally covered simply under the title of purpose of the research. In any case, PB taught students that all science begins with a hypothesis. NIH grant applications might, but science starts with curiosity. Anton van Leeuwenhook (1632–1723) did not build the microscope to discover bacteria and living organisms in a drop of swamp water to test a hypothesis. Newton's laws of motion were not formulated to test a hypothesis. As one scientist (Louis Katz) said at a meeting in 1950, the real value of science is to satisfy curiosity. In the book by Feynman, *The Pleasure of Finding Things Out* (1999), he got it right when he said (p. 248), "You investigate for curiosity, because it is unknown." The amazing thing is how a device like the microscope that was considered a curiosity hundreds of years ago is used today throughout the world as a diagnostic tool.

One obvious characteristic of science therefore is the change in our perception of nature that comes with new studies. In the 1930s we learned that there were ninety-three chemical elements, that hyenas were cowardly scavengers, and that Washington was the tallest mountain east of the Mississippi River. Since then, atomic scientists have made new chemical elements, documentaries prove hyenas are bold hunters, and surveys show that Mt. Mitchell is the tallest of the Appalachians. The discovery of new plants, animals, and chemical reactions seem endless. It is the acquisition of facts through curiosity that fuels the growth of science. Most academicians establish reputations for finding new facts in some special area of study, be it entomology, petroleum engineering, biochemistry, or countless other fields of endeavor. The tremendous advances in medicine have been due to better information, not better theories. Theories, hypotheses, inferences, extrapolations, and guesses (including teleology) are useful in organizing and explaining phenomena studied and provide paradigms for further investigation, but remain ideas unless substantiated by observation and experimentation.

The late Richard Feynman in his book *The Pleasure of Finding Things Out* (1999) correctly contends that government should not be empowered to decide on the validity of scientific theory. In the former Soviet Union the government did and Stalin personally embraced the agricultural theory of Trofin D. Lysenko in 1935. Later Krushchev did likewise. Lysenko was an uneducated farmer who had truck loads of soil moved to different areas to show that soil changed the nature of plants, among other "experiments." He denounced the established theories (biological explanations) of the likes of Mendel and Pasteur as drivel and silenced all academic opposition of biologists. His cronies were given degrees and Lysenko was honored by having statues erected to him. Lysenko controlled biological research and even suppressed new knowledge of the mother substance of life, DNA. However, by 1962 legitimate Soviet scientists began to surreptitiously publish genetic findings in journals otherwise devoted to physics, chemistry, and even mathematics. The academic scientists finally prevailed and an investigation showed the fraudulent nature of Lysenko's work, e.g., extra water was supplied to trees that presumably adapted to the desert environment. In October 1964, when Krushchev lost power, Lysenko was dismissed as director of the Institute of Genetics. But for nearly thirty years government had supported the politically correct ravings of an ignorant man.

Lawmakers in our democracy occasionally try, in their fashion, to decide on the merits of a scientific theory or fact. Many of them still hold to the adage that a million Frenchmen can't be wrong. But they can all be wrong concerning properties of cholinesterase. As discussed in the chapter "Evil Evolution," the teaching of evolution has been outlawed by state legislators and now a small group of scientific creationists try to force their theory to be taught by law. Here the zealot wants a theory to be endorsed by the legislature while in the former Soviet Union, Lysenko only needed the approval of one person. During the industrial revolution the State Legislature of Indiana in 1897 unanimously approved in both House and Senate a bill that required that the value of Pi be taught correctly as 3.0, not 3.1415 etc. Could so many learned men (women did not vote), including Dr. Goodman who introduced the bill, be wrong? This House Bill No. 246, which introduced a new mathematical truth, did not ultimately become law because a Professor Waldo of Purdue University happened to hear the bill debated before the second and final reading in the Senate (Peter Beckman, *A History of Pi*, St. Martin's Press, 1976). One of my college math professors, a woman, mentioned this incident to us to illustrate the harm ignorance may generate.

CHAPTER 9

Evil Evolution

NOTHING SEPARATES THE SERIOUS PUPIL OF SCIENCE FROM PRONOUNCEMENTS of the pulpit than evolution. As discussed later, many who have accepted the evidence of evolution have also embraced religious beliefs while the biblical inerrant dogmatist identifies evolution as an abomination to be eradicated. The controversy really began with the findings obtained by Charles Robert Darwin (1809–1882) while serving as a naturalist for five years on board H.M.S. *Beagle* that started in 1831. Darwin collected specimens of plants and animals, searched for fossils, and studied geology in the many countries the expedition visited. The facts he collected convinced the scientific world that evolution had occurred and he also proposed a theory to account for evolution—natural selection. In his day the laws of heredity and molecular biology were unknown; but he reasoned that if man can selectively breed for different kinds of dogs or horses, nature might do likewise over eons to create different species. In any case, his analysis of the living and the dead (fossils) convinced him and other scientists of evolution.

Modern methodology has revealed much concerning the mechanism of evolution and these are described in modern texts (e.g., *The Molecular Biology of the Cell*, 1994, Alberts et al.). However, many have rejected the facts and especially the theory of evolution after the publication of Darwin's first book in 1859. The most famous remonstrator in England was Bishop Wilberforce, who debated at Oxford the naturalist Thomas H. Huxley on the subject. The most famous confrontation on the subject occurred in Dayton, Tennessee, shortly after the state legislature passed a law in 1925 making it illegal to teach evolution. John Scopes was put on trial for breaking the law. William Jennings Bryan (1860–1925), who failed in three attempts to be president of the USA, was brought in as the prosecuting attorney. Clarence Darrow, a famous trial lawyer, defended Scopes. It was often called the monkey trial and the proceedings were depicted in the movie of 1960, *Inherit the Wind*, starring Spencer Tracy and Fredric March. Bryan died that year and since Scopes had broken the law, he was fined $100. Nevertheless, the courts seemed a strange place to debate teaching science and the law against teaching evolution was not rigorously enforced afterward. The law was finally repealed in 1967 by the Tennessee state legislature. But the controversy and monkey business lives on. When Pope John Paul II declared that evolution was more than a theory, one Italian newspaper declared that he "made peace with Darwin" while another wrote, "Pope says we descend from monkeys" (CA 10/25/96).

The layman's prejudicial view of evil evolution is exemplified by an article written by Cal Thomas (CA 8/29/02). He tells us that high school students should be taught creationism with evolution to "allow students to decide which view makes sense." High school texts can only summarize the discoveries of science. To understand the evidence for evolution students (and teachers) would study for years embryology, comparative anatomy, molecular biology, geology, paleontology, paleoanthropology, chemistry, physics, and whatever. They would need the same evidence to accept or refute creationism. Thomas laments that evolution leaves God out of the picture and cites two dead physicists that acknowledged His existence. Perhaps Thomas would have science texts acknowledge that God made sodium chloride, gravity, the lever, the electron, valences, evolution, and all things. Thomas likes the Christian creationists who write that a great flood killed the dinosaurs, created our Grand Canyon in several days, and deposited the remains of ocean creatures miles high into the Andes. Thomas dislikes the "reputable scientists" of the world who dismiss such claims and he argues that they are only defending their academic influence. Indeed, the title of his article is "Evolutionists Bare Their Fears." The whole article implies that all evolutionists are atheists and are afraid of anyone who attacks their evidence. Evolutionists are also Christians, Moslems, Hindus, and members of other faiths. Thomas thought that the "wave of books" recently written by creationists added credibility to their view but did not say whether he studied them or the books written to refute the creationism that has been so avidly embraced by some Christian faiths. He even argues that the views expressed by creationists are rejected by academic scholars because they believe in God and put

Him in the evidence. But the work of the dead physicists mentioned by Thomas was applauded by reputable scientists even though the physicists believed in God. Thomas is a successful wordmonger who could not discern that opinion was not science to advise high school students.

Other laymen speaking at school board meetings are more succinct than Thomas. One in Georgia said, "Evolution is strictly a theory, and we don't think it should be taught as fact" (CA 8/23/02). This is a standard cliché. The school board was considering whether to teach creationism with evolution to expose students to "a wide and objective range of ideas." At least one parent voiced the view that creationism was deception, but the debate goes on in California, Indiana, Kansas, Ohio, and elsewhere. The creationists have essentially rewritten Genesis using terms provided by reputable scientists. Fundamentalists embrace their theory regardless of the facts.

Thousands of pulpits and hundreds of teachers denounce evolution. The four chapters herein that dealt with the books of Genesis makes the reasons for this vilification self-evident. Those who adamantly oppose evolution are variously called fundamentalists, literalists, or evangelicals and declare that every sentence in the Bible is accurate historically and scientifically. John Wesley (1703–1791) wrote on the subject "if there is one error in Scripture there might be a thousand. It would not be the truth of God." John Calvin (1509–1564) similarly wrote that the Bible is the pure word of God and the infallible rule of his holy truth. Many Christian denominations adhere to this doctrine of biblical inerrancy, such as the Berean Fundamental Church, Conservative Congregational Conference, and the Apostolic Christian Church of America (*Handbook of Denominations in the United States*, F.S. Mead, S.S. Hill, 1995). Apparently the largest single group of Christian fundamentalists, with a membership of 15.8 million, is the Southern Baptist Convention (CA 3/25/00). Biblical inerrancy is a serious business for millions and their voices are heard in schools and courtrooms.

Brian H. Edwards of the Hooks Evangelical Church, Surbiton, Surrey, England, wrote a book on evangelicalism for the layman that exemplifies the controversy. The title of the book, *Nothing but The Truth* (1993), summarizes his position and was alluded to in the chapters on Genesis. Edwards accepts the calculation by Archbishop James Ussher showing that creation began 4004 B.C. because it is based on "the absolute reliability of biblical dates" (p56). He rejects the conclusion of the archeologist Sr. Leonard Woolley in 1929 that the

Great Flood of the Bible was 400 miles long because the biblical flood covered all mountains with six meters of water and Noah was instructed to take all animals aboard his ship to save them (p. 288). Moreover, everybody today comes from Noah's family (p. 123). Edwards discusses in scholarly fashion that the Bible was written over a span of about 1500 years (p. 1), that all of the original writings were lost, that no handwriting of the authors of the Bible exist (p. 175), and that "in fact, we have some 20,000 different sources to help us, and at times confuse us, in our search for an accurate text for the New Testament" (p. 197). He further discusses some of the problems of translating Hebrew, Aramaic, and Greek into English and in the selection of an English version. As a biblical scholar, Edwards points out some inaccuracies and deficiencies in these versions. Yet he argues that men wrote accurately of events that happened long before their time (p. 296) and praises the articles of faith issued by The Chicago Statement on Biblical Inerrancy in 1977 (p. 341). In Article XII they deny any science that may overturn the Scripture on creation and the flood (p. 351). The pontificating men (women are not mentioned) of the Chicago Statement say, with humility, that agreeing with them is a mark of true Christianity. With regard to evolution, Edwards states that, "if we listen to false scientists and assume our ancestors were monkeys, then we will behave like monkeys" (p. 337). He also uses the cliché that "evolution is a theory that no scientist can prove" and laments that many evangelicals fail to know the difference between scientific facts and theory (p. 15). How much embryology, comparative anatomy, paleontology, geology, astrophysics, and molecular biology, or any science that Edwards studied is unknown, but he easily identifies false scientists. He makes it clear that "hasty theories" that come in the name of science must be tested by Scripture and that "an inerrant Bible submits to no man' s judgment" (p. 44). Millions apparently subscribe to this biblical inerrant dogma for the reason Edwards presents in three words: People want authority (p. 45). But real science is not about authority; it is about discovery.

Another group that actively opposes evolution refer to themselves as scientific creationists. The group has members who hold advanced degrees in various sciences, like biology and geology, and are conversant with the basic facts of evolution and newer findings that alter the old Darwinian hypothesis. As supporter of the Creation Science Research Center of San Diego, California, they publish biology textbooks that present their view of how natural phenomena started which resembles the biblical account of creation. To my knowledge this is the only scientific group that recruits preachers, legislators, and educators to support their conclusions and even initiate lawsuits to have their theory taught (*Science*, Vol. 211:1331–32, 1981). *A* recent poll indicated that while 83 percent supported the teaching of evolution, a majority (79 percent) also felt that creationism had a place in the public school curriculum (CA 3/11/00). The literature and videos dealing with scientific creationism have been available for some thirty years.

The public school edition of *Scientific Creationism*, edited by H.M. Morris, Ph.D. (Creation-Life Publisher, San Diego, California, 1974), that was prepared by the technical staff and consultants for the Institute of Creation Science summarizes for high school biology teachers their critique of evolution. Their account of creation differs from the inerrant biblical account in being less specific. For instance, they state that the various tribes and languages known today stem from survivors of the worldwide flood (p. 187), not from Noah's immediate family, and that these survivors started civilization in the region of Mount Ararat or Babylon "where the confusion of languages took place" (p. 188). Their description of a great flood as a hydraulic cataclysm (water gushed from underground aquifers) when "sooner or later all land animals would perish" while some humans "managed to ride out the cataclysm in unusually strong watertight sea-going vessels" (p. 117), certainly differs from the biblical account of Noah's experiences. They accept the archeological data that humans made figurines by 9,000 B.C. (p. 189) but by an analysis of the decay of the earth's magnetic field (p. 157), the influx meteoric material from space (p. 151), and by discrediting modern methods of dating the age of materials on earth, they concluded the age of the earth to be at most 10,000 years (p. 158) or 8,000 B.C. onward. By their analysis, figurines were being made at least 1,000 years before the earth was formed, but they make no claim of being inerrant scientists. They are scientists fighting for Christianity.

The scientific creationists also tell the high school teacher that the labeling of geologic time and formations (found in most dictionaries) is correct except for the time from Archeozoic (same as Precambrian) through Pleistocene and recent (p. 129). The effect of the great flood was initially seen as sedimentary deposits during the Proterozoic (same as late Precambrian) era and ended in the Teriary Period as the "Final phase of the Flood, along with initial phases of the post-Flood readjustments" (p. 129). Their cataclysmic (flood) model—the sudden release of tremendous subterranean forces (p. 128)—and their analysis of dendrochronology, carbon dating, etc. lead the creationists to conclude that "man's new start after the global cataclysm" to be around 4,000 to 6,000 years B.C. (p. 193).

Since most biology teachers also never formally studied paleoanthropology, Chapter VII of the text covers the terminology of that field of science, such as hominid. The creationists dismiss many of the hominids as extinct monkeys that other scientists consider to be associated with the beginnings of the human form. A more human-like extinct hominid, *Homo erectus*, creationists conjecture, was a true man, most likely a decadent descendant "because of inbreeding, poor diet, and a hostile environment" and whose genes lingered in Australia (p. 174). This too does not resemble the biblical account of Noah and his descendants. They agree with academic paleoanthropologists that Neanderthal (or Neandertal) man was a true human being, not a missing link in evolution, but looked like an ape relative to us because he suffered from rickets during his stay on earth (p. 175). Neanderthal man (*Homo neanderthalensis*) may well have suffered from rickets (Scandinavians learned to use cod liver oil to prevent rickets), but he was more bony and more muscular than us (caveman-like), and the author of the article the creationists indirectly cited (F. Ivanhoe, *Nature*, Vol. 227:577-79, 1970) discusses his findings in evolutionary terms. Ironically the same year that the creationist book was published (1974), Donald Johanson discovered Lucy, and later her close relatives, who has become a famous human ancestral fossil 3 million to 4 million years old. Very recently two students noted that Lucy's family (*Australopithecus afarensis*) have a ridge on the radius bone that prevents the wrist from rocking backward which is present in the great apes (gorilla etc.). The ridge is not found in hominid fossils that academics identity as our more recent ancestors, such as *Australopithecus africanus* and *Homo habilis*, nor in us (CA 3/26/00). The book by D. Johanson, B. Edger, and photographer D. Brill (*From Lucy to Language*, 1996) seems to summarize nicely current thought and past findings of academic paleoanthropologists. This coffee table-size book features color photographs of over fifty specimens of the most significant early hominid fossils, in actual size, together with the skulls of modern man for comparison. The photos gave me the eerie feeling of looking back in time.

Nevertheless, the scientific creationists make it clear to the high school teacher that all living things were created essentially at the same time, being "created contemporaneously by the Creator" (p.117). "Both bats and birds needed wings to fly, so the Creator created wings for both of them" (p.75), and dinosaurs were contemporary with man as evidenced by footprints that overlap in central Texas, footprints in stone (p. 122). The obvious reason why human bones have not been found among the thousands of dinosaur fossils is because man would naturally avoid them as he does crocodiles today (p. 117). The purpose of the eye is for seeing, they reason, and there is no need to assume that the eye of man evolved from fish (p. 34). The purpose of having cavefish that have no eyes at all, yet thrive in eternal darkness in limestone caverns, escapes me. Also, the spring cavefish (*Chologaster agassizi*) has eyes but if removed still does very well (*Wondrous World of Fishes*, Nat. Geo. Soc., 1965). However, an appeal of scientific creationism is that the moon, stars, and everything has a purpose (pp. 32–35). They agree that mutations may occur, which would explain the degenerative functions of some tissue like the nictitating membrane, appendix, and earlobe muscles of humans that the evolutionists have mistaken for vestigial tissue in man, but important to other species (p. 76). Moreover, they claim there are far more harmful genetic mutations than good ones so that mutations could play no role in producing new organisms that thrive as conjectured by the evolutionists (pp. 56, 67, 181). Mathematically they show that man could not have lived on earth as long as the evolutionists state because of population growth statistics (p. 167). If so, we would be dead from crowding by now. David Feldman in his *Hallmark Book on Imponderables* (1988) also wonders why the earth is not covered with horse flies when a single pair could produce 326 trillion offspring in one summer (p. 134).

Isaac Newton is often cited as an immortal man of science who spent much time studying Scripture and believed in God. This genius also wrote that religion and philosophy (science) "are to be preserved distinct." Moreover, he said, "We are not to introduce divine revelations into philosophy nor philosophical opinions into religion" (*Sir Isaac Newton* by H.D. Anthony, Collier Books, 1960). The creationists depict Newton as a religious scientist studying God's work, but they ignore his admonition to separate science and religion in their biblical version of the origin of life on earth.

The scientific creationists declare that their model of the universe is based on the premise that what started it all was supernatural (p. 12). The first cause (as in cause and effect) was the Creator that they identify as a male: "the Creator to sustain and maintain the basic systems He had created" (p. 12). By their analysis they show that the data collected independently by astronomers, geologists, and naturalists for many years disprove the conclusions of the evolutionists and astrophysicists

(p. 13). Creationists sell videos to show that dinosaurs and the earth are a few thousand years old (*Parade* section, CA 8/9/98). They appeal to teachers to consider fairly their conclusion that the earth and universe are of recent origin, not billions of years old (p. 137). While there are many recently published books that deal with the nuances of evolution, such as *Cells, Embryos and Evolution* by J. Gerhart / M. Kirscher, 1997, and *Darwinian Dynamics* by R.E. Michod, 1999, Carl Baugh, Ph.D., has written the definitive book to refute the evolutionists titled *Why Do Men Believe Evolution Against All Odds?*, 1999. Women apparently are all nonbelievers. Dr. Baugh is founder and Director of the Creation Evidence Museum, Glen Rose, Texas. His conclusions, again, are that organisms appeared on earth fully formed on an earth that is only thousands of years old. Then He too started it all. On the other hand, Gerald L. Schroeder in his book *The Science of God*, 1997, starts with life beginning some 3.8 billion years ago (p. 129) and explains, as a distinguished physicist and biblical scholar, how the modern findings of biochemists, paleontologists, astrophysicists, and other sciences are compatible with biblical teachings. There are even books recently written by academics to refute the creationists: *Tower of Babel*, by Robert T. Pennock (1999) and *The Triumph of Evolution*. by Niles Eldridge (2000).

So, the scientific creationists are at odds with the biblical inerrant scholars, with the academic evolutionists, and with a distinguished religious physicist. The fundamentalists would abolish evolution by law and the creationists would have their theory taught by law.

CHAPTER 10

Theocratic Politics

THEOCRACY IS NOT A BIBLICAL WORD, BUT THE IDEA THAT GOD SHOULD DIRECT human behavior is biblical. In early biblical times He ruled directly through men such as Moses, Aaron, and Joshua, then later by using a group called judges. These judges were mainly a series of military leaders who rose to fight enemies of the nation of Israel, the last being Samson. These were troubled times because too many Israelis would periodically worship false gods and everyone did what was right in their own eyes (Judges 17:6; 21:25).

Then, about 1050 B.C. the Israelis adopted kings, of which Saul was the first. When one of his subjects, the hero David, killed a giant Philistine in combat, Saul became worried that David might replace him as king and planned to have him murdered. Eventually David became king, but only of Judah. The rest of the Israelis elected the son of Saul, Ishbosheth, as their king. When Ishbosheth was murdered (assassinated), David became king of the nation of Israel. God prevented David from building a house of worship but could not prevent him from committing adultery with Bathsheba. It is unlikely that Solomon, David's son, ever committed adultery as he had 700 wives and 300 concubines (1 Kings 11:3). As king, Solomon was an astute leader, Israel prospered, and the famous temple was built. Twice Solomon saw God (1 Kings 9:1–9), who gave him religious instruction that was largely ignored. The three books in our Bible that he reportedly wrote are replete with cogent comments on human behavior, excellent advice, and loving thoughts, as well as disturbing words. We learn from him that one rotten apple can spoil a barrelful (Ecclesiastes 9:18, TLB), that students are wise who master what their teachers tell them (Ecclesiastes 12:11, TLB) and, in his Song of Solomon, about the joy of being in love where kisses are sweeter than wine. In Proverbs we are told that wise men use common sense (17:21, TLB), and that the first step to wisdom is in reverence and trust of God (1:7–8, TLB). If so, his subjects seemed to be largely devoid of godliness and common sense, for Solomon found that no women and only one man per thousand were wise (Ecclesiastes 7:28, TLB).

For about 400 years God's children, chosen to do good, were led mainly by kings who chose to do bad. Their reigns are summarized in our Bibles for King Jehoram, who was as wicked as the other kings of Israel (2 Kings 8:18, KJV). The Assyrians ended the experiment with kings for Israel in 722 B.C. Later Judah fell to Babylon in 586 B.C. and the temple Solomon built for God was destroyed.

Theocratic politics has been also important in the history of other nations. The emperors of Japan, for instance, traced their lineage back to Ninigi, grandson of the Shinto sun goddess, and were considered divine by millions until January 1, 1946, when Emperor Hirohito declared otherwise. His son, Akihito, was enthroned as emperor in 1990.

In old Russia, the czar was head of government and Christianity. This relationship was symbolically depicted in their emblem featuring a two-headed eagle. The two-headed monster did not serve Christ or government very well and was replaced in 1917 by the atheistic government of communism. Its first dictator, Nikolai Lenin (1870–1924), commented that "religion is the opium of the people," apparently dulling the senses or good sense, and churches were closed. If the people had known the Bible, they may have saved the czar for Paul tells us that "every person be subject to government authority" and explains that we are to pay taxes and so forth (Romans 13:1–7, KJV). Peter similarly admonishes us to be subject to every human institution, whether emperor or governors (1 Peter 2:13–14, KJV). Jesus likewise separated belief from what belongs to Caesar (Matthew 22:17–21, KJV). He even said that the secular governor Pilate was given power from above to try him (John 19:11, KJV). The idea of supporting secular government is ignored by some Christian denominations in not voting or taking oaths, etc., while I have recently heard some religious leaders link Christianity to patriotism and the founding of America. Nathanael Greene (1742–1780) was disowned by members of his Quaker faith for becoming one of our greatest generals of the Revolutionary War. He was trusted by Washington and the troops he led, and for that even the Quakers are proud (*Friends in the Carolinas*, J.F. Moore, 1971). But General Greene, Patrick Henry, and our other Founding Fathers fought for liberty, not religion. Like the last czar of Russia, Nicholas II, they had a religion before the revolution and were even free to be a noncombatant Quaker. Religion did not serve Nicholas or Russia well.

The government established by the Puritans, also called Pilgrims, who arrived near Boston in 1620 is a good example of a microtheocracy in America. These Puritans left England for religious reasons to Holland where they were able to worship as they chose. They then went to Massachusetts and we laud their determination to suffer much to worship in their manner. Once here theocracy took hold. The preacher Roger Williams was expelled for declaring that people should not be punished for religious differences. When two Quakers, Mary Fisher and Ann Austin, arrived in Boston in 1656, they were stripped and searched for marks of witchcraft on their bodies and later sent in exile to Barbados. Apparently the Puritan God did not like Quakers for Mary Dyer was hanged on Boston Common in 1660. I understand that she was executed while tied to a chair. Other Quakers hanged by these theocrats were Marmaduke Stephensen and William Robinson in 1659, and William Ledra in 1661 (*Walk Cheerfully, Friends* by S.B. Hinshaw, 1978). Many Quakers died in prison to keep the Puritans pure. Eventually King Charles II, who in 1660 came to power after the religious terror imposed by the Puritan Oliver Cromwell, decreed an end to executions for religious reasons. Some believe that the atrocious behavior of the Puritans and the example set by Williams for religious inclusion contributed significantly to the concept of the separation of church and state.

Another example of microtheocracy in America was initiated by Joseph Fielding Smith, (1805–1844), who started at age twenty-five the Church of Jesus Christ of Latter-day Saints in 1830. He was obviously a handsome male who had wrestled for sport as a youth and had also sinned (*Truth Restored*, Gordon Hinckley, 1979; *Joseph Smith Tells His Own Story*, circa 1950). He sought religion and was partial to the Methodist sect but when he prayed to God for guidance, he saw two from heaven and one said, "This is my Beloved Son, hear Him." Smith was told not to join any existing church as all were corrupt. Later the angel Moroni visited him and told him where to find some gold plates, which he had to translate, that restored the Bible as the Book of Mormon. The gold plates also revealed the origins of our native Americans. Moreover, Smith wrote that Peter, James, and John sent John the Baptist from heaven to ordain him as a priest. Smith was brilliant and soon led a religious group that was cooperative and successful. Their success and independence was offensive to many outsiders (the gentiles) and Smith had to move his group many times prior to his death in Illinois. In Illinois he was offered land where he established the city of Nauvoo, which with about 20,000 inhabitants was the largest in the state with much voting clout in the 1840s. Here his influence was great as mayor, lieutenant general of his military, and as president of the church where his revelations were law. He also announced on June 7, 1844, that he was running for president of the USA. One revelation he kept secret for years was "celestial marriage, which others called polygamy." It was hard to keep this secret and Smith informed the group in 1842 of his doctrine of celestial marriage. In 1844 some Mormons finally remonstrated and published a newspaper article critical of polygamy and of Smith's autocratic rule. The press was demolished, some say by a secret organization called Danites named after members of the army of David (1 Chronicles 12:35). So went freedom of the press in the community of Nauvoo. Smith and his brother were arrested for ordering the destruction of the press and jailed in a nearby city, Carthage, where both were killed by a mob on June 27, 1844. Whether his militia failed to obey his orders to rescue him is controversial (*A Gathering of Saints*, Robert Lindsey, 1988). In any case, Smith at thirty-nine years left forty-nine wives by one account. The Mormons of Nauvoo were then terribly persecuted and driven from Illinois. A real genius, Brigham Young, led many from Nauvoo to Utah where in 1852 he made public polygamy by the Mormon Church. He had only twenty-seven wives. Our Supreme Court took issue with the practice and to gain statehood for Utah, Church President Wilford Woodruff in 1890 declared by revelation the end of plural marriages for Mormons. The practice started and ended with revelation (*Truth Restored*, 1979). By many accounts, Mormons today promote strong healthy family ties, eagerly serve their country, and the few I have known were exemplary. But remnants of the early days seem to persist as seen in the investigation of murder (*A Gathering of Saints*, R. Lindsey, 1988), in bigamy in Utah (CA 5/19/01), and with the type of laws passed by 70 percent of the citizens of Utah who are Mormons. One disgruntled lawyer stated that Utah was founded as a theocracy and remains a theocracy (CA 3/11/01).

John Alexander Dowie was another theocrat who in 1901 founded a religious community in Illinois named Zion City (just north of Chicago). Dowie was head of the Christian Catholic Church which he started. He had some good social ideals and became famous for healing disease through prayer. Later he claimed to be the prophet Elijah restored and in 1906 was disposed as leader. Zion is no longer a theocracy (*Handbook of Denominations*. F.S. Mead, S.S. Hill, 1995).

Microtheocracy is clearly evident in Hasidism in America (*A Life Apart*, TV documentary, PBS, WKNO, Memphis, 4/15/02). Men and women worship separately and boys and girls attend private schools separately to study the five books of Moses—the Pentateuch or Torah. Movies, TV, pop music, and sports are forbidden and none may study at our universities, as these are impure. None become doctors or lawyers but business is permitted. The adult male Hasidim has a beard and wears dark clothing and everything is a spiritual act done for God, including having large families. The head of their societal hierarchy is the "Rebbe" (Yiddish for "Rabbi") and arriving in the USA after WWII by ship, one said that they would tailor America to fit the Torah. Unlike the Amish, they use modern electrical appliances, buses, trains, airplanes, cellular phones and other products of impurity from the outside world. The rebbe is not only a spiritual leader, he is king and flag to his followers, it was said. Leaders of the ultra-Orthodox Jews of Israel have the reputation of using politics to extract funds to support their schools and large religious families. The Israeli Prime Minister Ariel Sharon recently got fed up with their selfish demands and fired members of the Shas and United Torah parties who were serving in his cabinet (CA 5/22/02). Theocracy serves some well.

John Calvin (1509–1564) was a great religious leader who also considered government as an instrument of religion. He was reared as a Roman Catholic but elected to join the Reformation. He fled his homeland France to Switzerland when Francois I decided his country would remain loyal to the French traditions of Catholicism. So much for religious freedom. Calvin landed in Geneva and with others formed a political party that demanded high morals. He was expelled in 1538 but returned in 1541 when his reform party took control. Most entertainment was forbidden and special agents called "presbyters" were appointed to impose moral conduct on the citizens. When another Protestant leader, Michael Servetus, came to Geneva for asylum, Calvin had Servetus tried as a heretic and burned alive at the stake.

In all of Christendom the Roman Catholics have the longest record of theocracy and misuse of power. Bishop Fulton J. Sheen was a Roman Catholic who wrote a brief but realistic history of his church for the *World Book Encyclopedia* (1960) that mentions the corruption initiated by many popes and their minions. *Halley's Bible Handbook* (H.H. Halley, 1965) describes in more detail the unsavory acts perpetuated by Catholics, and the *Encyclopedia Britannica* (1945) contains biographies of many unscrupulous popes.

Catholic theocracy became entrenched under the Western Roman Emperor Constantine the Great (A.D. 272–337) who took the cross as a battle symbol after having a vision that said, "By this cross thou shall conquer." He defeated the Roman Emperor of the East, Licinius, moved the Roman capital east, and named it Constantinople (now Istanbul). Afterwards Christians received favorable treatment among religions of the empire, and to settle a theological dispute among Christian bishops about Trinity, Constantine called a council of churchmen to Nicaea from which came our Nicene Creed, designed to unite Christendom forever. In those days no church leader was known as a pope, but under Constantine Christianity became a state religion while Silvester I (314–335) was bishop of Rome. At that time Silvester and others governed church matters as patriarchs with equal authority. After the death of Constantine (337), churchman from the western part of the empire met at Sardica in 343 and recognized the Roman bishop, Julius I (337–352), as their authority. However, the Roman bishops had difficulty ruling Christians living eastward, especially after the empire divided into east and west in 395. About then Siricius (385–398) claimed universal jurisdiction in church matters. Shortly after another Roman bishop, Innocent I (402–417), called himself "Ruler of the Church of God." Pope Leo I (440–461) became a hero when he persuaded Attila the Hun and Genseric the Vandal not to plunder Rome. He proclaimed himself "Lord of the Whole Church" and advocated death for heresy.

By the time Gregory I (590–604) became a pope, people were purchasing church titles (simony) and power. But Gregory was a good guy who fought simony and oppression, helped the poor, and converted England to Christianity. Since popes do not usually live long as rulers, their influence dies with them. Many popes who followed Gregory were declared immoral by their bishops. Benedict IX (1024—1035) became a pope at age twelve by simony and was eventually driven from Rome because of gross immorality. Pope Leo X (1513–1521) became an archbishop at age eight, and simony continued. With Nicholas I (858—867), popes began to wear a crown. Our early Christian leaders then had a crown, a throne, a coat of arms, and power like other kings. No wonder Saint Peter worried that future leaders of Christianity might lord it over others (1 Peter 5:3).

The power popes had in civil matters reached zenith under Innocent III. There were actually two Innocent III popes, one nine years before the other. The first was elected by opponents of Alexander III for 1179–1180, but Alexander bribed his supporters and the first one was jailed. Since the first Innocent III lost, he is classified as one of many anti-popes. The second Innocent III (1198–1216) was a scholar from the noble family of count Segni, Italy. Although he was not a priest at the time, he was unanimously elected pope and astutely took control of Europe. One sovereign was forced to take back his divorced wife and another to divorce his wife because the couple were too closely related.

Innocent III used crusades to make change. Eastern Catholics were subdued after a bloody siege of Constantinople in 1204 and a westerner, Thomas Morocini, made patriarch. Innocent III declared that members of the Christian sects called Albigenses (named after a French town, Albi) and Waldenese (named after a Frenchman, Waldo) as heretics to be exterminated. A crusade started in 1208 eventually killed all of the thousands that belonged to these sects, except for a few Waldenese. He also initiated another crusade in 1218 to control Jerusalem with poor results. When King John (1199– 1216) refused to accept Stephen Langton as Archbishop of Canterbury, Innocent III suspended all religious observances in England—baptism, marriages, burial, etc. When John then seized all church revenues, he was excommunicated and threatened with a crusade. The two eventually made peace by John resigning his kingdom to Innocent and agreeing to buy it back with English money that was paid to popes for over a century. But he obtained absolution with this monetary tribute. However, Innocent totally governed England during the last years of King John and the early years of Henry III through his representatives (legates).

One of the least known, but remarkable, crusades to win Jerusalem for Christianity was lead by Frederick II, king of Sicily and Germany, and under Pope Honorius III was Holy Roman Emperor (1220). He was reared under the protection of Innocent III and at an early age promised a crusade. His crusade was delayed for years and by the time he went a new pope, Gregory IX, in anger excommunicated him. Since the king had lost his Christianity, Gregory sent his papal soldiers to occupy the territories of Frederick and gained new revenue for himself. In the meantime, Frederick with his army met Sultan Malik-al-Adil and by friendly diplomacy acquired control of lands that Richard the Lionhearted had previously failed to acquire by conquest. Frederick crowned himself king of Jerusalem, returned to Italy, destroyed the papal armies, and secured absolution from the same but humbler Pope Gregory IX (1229). As a heretic this king peacefully opened Jerusalem for Christians and by brute force restored his Christianity.

The Inquisition was another manifestation of the power our early Christian brethren had in civil affairs. Historians tell us it started with Emperor Constantine (306–337) when the teachings of the Christian Church were considered fundamental to law and order. To be a non-believer of these teachings became an offense against the state and the church. Clergymen conducted the investigation in secret and the accused did not know who testified against them. Torture of men, women, children, and slaves was permitted to obtain information concerning heresy. When found guilty, the punishment might be monetary, the confiscation of land and goods, loss of hereditary rights, exile, or death. Civilian authorities carried out the punishment. Priscillian of Spain, for instance, was executed for heresy in 385 by the Roman emperor Maximus. Pope Innocent III (1190–1216) is said to have perfected the use of the Inquisition for secular power. Eventually this instrument of religious power waned with the rise of many Christian denominations and in 1834 the branch of Roman Catholicism, called The Holy Office, ceased to investigate heretics by inquisition.

Even years after the Reformation of the 1500s, the Pope was absolute ruler of much territory. However, by 1860 Pope Pius IX only controlled land in central Italy called the Papal States. Then Victor Immanuel II, king of Italy, took over most of that land. However, Pius IX housed, fed, and paid 10,000 French troops to protect Rome, but these soldiers returned to France in 1870 because of war with Germany, and Rome was taken by force that same year. By free election the Italians chose Rome to be their secular capital. Traditional papal theocracy is now confined to the 108.7 acres of Vatican City, ruled by a pope. It is the smallest nation on earth.

Islam has been called an empire of faith and is an example of theocracy in practice today. This great religion started with the Arab Hadkrat Mohammed (A.D. 570–632), variously spelled Muhammad and Mohomet. He was orphaned at six, reared by an uncle and others, and became familiar with Jewish and Christian teachings, and embraced some ideas of each. Prior to Mohammed, Arabs did not believe in a hereafter or heaven, worshiped many idols—sort of for good luck—and killed unwanted baby girls. Mohammed changed this. He knew he was on the right tract when Gabriel, the same angel that visited our Virgin Mary, told him on many occasions what to teach in the city of Mecca. But he was driven from Mecca in 622 for radical ideas. In the city of Medina (Yathrib), however, he patiently won the hearts of the people and they made him king and theocracy started. He built the first mosque there, led prayers of worship, and established traditional religious services for his followers, the Moslems (Muslims). His followers held off a greater army sent from Mecca to destroy Mohammed, indicating that Allah (God) was on their side. While Mohammed preached the Ten Commandments and emphasized charity for the poor and orphaned, the practice of theocracy by force was introduced when the Moslems conquered their enemies in Mecca. Upon his death in 632, the Moslems elected several able leaders (caliph) to carry on his work, the first being Abu Bekr (Bakr), a wealthy merchant. Islam then spread far and wide. One hundred years after his death, Moslem soldiers almost entered Paris, but were defeated at Tours in 732 by forceful Franks who took advantage of a quarrel among Moslem generals. The second caliph, Omar, took Jerusalem in 638 by defeating the soldiers of Byzantine Roman Catholic General Heracles, who only nine years before (629) took the city from Persia. Omar was dismayed that holy sites were in ruin and used as city dumps. Not long after conquering Jerusalem, Omar was murdered by a lowly Persian slave in 644.

For many centuries Islam prospered under great leadership and fostered scholarship. Their scholars embraced history, the sciences—for they saw no conflict between natural law and religion as did the early Roman Catholics—architecture, invention, and gave us Arabic numerals. Jewish and Christian scholars were welcomed in Baghdad and elsewhere to share their expertise. It is said that these Moslem scholars were indispensable to the future of European culture by preserving early history and by innovations like the high vaulted ceilings of great buildings and the bank check to expedite business. Their mathematics and astronomy reigned supreme. But theocracies often deviate from the course set by the religious founders as they are governed by human whim, as are dictatorships. About nine hundred years from the start of the Islamic calendar (622), Suleiman the Magnificent (1494–1566) was born. Suleiman unified civil law for all Moslems, murdered two of his Moslem sons and best friend because he thought their success threatened his power and Islam, killed the king of Hungary in 1526, and nearly took Vienna. Scholarship was not his goal.

Meanwhile Christians were killing each other. In 1527 some unpaid German soldiers of the Vatican pillaged Rome and as a refugee Pope Clement VII paid the troops to leave the city. The German religious wars began the same year Martin Luther died in 1546. And the unarmed Protestant Huguenots, who bad worked peacefully in France for years, were slaughtered by order of King Charles IX in 1572 on the Holy Day of Saint Bartholomew.

While disputes over scientific theories may be intense, it is interesting that theological disputes may be deadly or result in religious schisms that last. Although Mohammad said that the ink of the scholar is more valuable than the blood of the martyr, as early as 699 the Moslem scholar Mabad al-Juhana was put to death as a heretic for teaching that men have power over their own actions rather than everything being predestined. The 1980–1988 war between the Moslem nations of Iran and Iraq resembles the carnage seen in earlier wars among Christians. The leaders of each nation played on different aspects of Islam to justify the war. Iraq started by shelling a border town of Iran in April 1980 and even killed 4,000 people of Halabja with chemical bombs. But Iran sent missiles to Baghdad, forced a cease-fire by 1988, and eventually forced Iraq to accept all of their terms to end the war officially in 1990. Then Iraq slaughtered the Moslems of Kuwait to start the so-called Desert Storm war of 1991.

Even ancient Greece struggled with theocracy while Socrates asked whether morality can exist without supernatural beliefs They also wrestled with the conflict between science and religion and at times religion won. One Greek philosopher, Protagoras, had his books burned and was banished from Athens for being uncertain about the gods. Astronomy was forbidden because it was contrary to religion (*The Life of Greece*, Will Durant, 1939). A soul left the body upon death but most went to Hades. The ancient gods may have promoted morality but they have all died. As the late mythologist Joseph Campbell explained, a dead religion becomes myth. Perhaps theocracy is an attempt by some to confirm that their religion is alive, for if the other religion is right, maybe theirs is wrong.

One consequence of religious schism within a given faith is that the development of the monstrous theocracies of the past is unlikely. A thorough mix of religions may have contributed to the religious tolerance I experienced in my hometown, near Chicago. Across the street from my home was a Greek Orthodox Church that was separated from a Roman Catholic Church only by a cinder-covered playing field. There seemed to be at least one church on every other block and on Sunday the ring of church bells was deafening. A synagogue was built next to my uncle's home, and it was said that the children in our schools represented thirty-one nations and about as many religions. Poverty was rampant in the 1930s, yet nearly all children dutifully attended church and school discipline was excellent. I would often attend church with my Roman Catholic friends, who never missed church, and found the experience gratifying. Once I attended a pleasant midnight Christmas service with a friend at a little Swedenborgian church (established in 1685 by Emmanuel Swedenborg). There were some cruel children and occasional fights, but more importantly children from many religious denominations played and learned together. In school we pledged allegiance to the flag, learned Lincoln's Gettysburg address, and silently faced east for one minute on Armistice Day (November 11) to honor the casualties of World War I. We respected each other and mourned for those who died so young in World War II, as well as for classmates who died later, regardless of their religion. As students we got along well without studying religion or praying in school.

While colossal theocracies may be a thing of the past, theocracy persists in some nations today and exist as microtheocracies in some communities. It certainly was evident in the middle of this past century, for I remember visiting the home of a college friend in Huntingburg, Indiana, and learned that only Protestants were hired to teach in their public schools while Jasper, a rival city seven miles away, only hired Catholics. Such religious discrimination was also evident in some of the small towns in Kansas where my wife taught several years shortly after World War II. And it was common knowledge that Jews need not apply—even at many of our major institutes of higher learning. It was as though to strengthen one religious denomination required debasing another. My introduction to this principle occurred as a boy when a Jewish family rented an apartment upstairs to ours and one playmate asked me how we could live so close to people who killed Christ. Confused, I asked my mother the same question and she said Roman soldiers killed Christ many years ago and not the people upstairs. But I have known Orthodox Jews who look askance at their Reform (even Conservative) brethren and that is certainly evident in Israel today where Reform rabbis can not perform any wedding ceremony (CA 3/22/00) and are angrily denounced if they visit the holy Western (Wailing) Wall in Jerusalem (CA 2/3/99). Israeli law prohibits vehicular travel on the Sabbath (CA 8/15/99) and the ultra-religious haredim, who dress somewhat like the Amish, are exempt by law from service in the armed forces, from work, and from taxes (CA 6/29/98). But the Orthodox feel free to call Israeli politicians Satan (CA 3/22/00) and declare that Jews killed during Nazi Germany were reincarnated sinners subject to atonement (CA

8/7/00). In Israel today nuns on Mt. Carmel never leave their cloister established in 1892 to pray for the reconciliation of hearts (CA 3/25/99). They are apparently still trying, but it is a major task; for Jerusalem has been historically a slaughterhouse for religion which today offers an abundance of hateful piety, plenty of faith but little hope, and more holy days than there are days of the year (CA 3/19/00).

But there is some hope in reports that many who live in Jerusalem of different faiths respect one another. Religious leaders are apparently important as seen in Roman Catholicism. In 1870 when Pope Pius IX (1848–1878) was forced to confine his temporal authority to only 108.7 acres, he declared that the separation of church and state was abominable, that Protestantism was not Christian, and that his pronouncements were infallible. Some German Roman Catholic priests refused to accept papal infallibility and they were excommunicated. So, these German priests founded the Old Catholic Church in 1871 and today some 500,000 hold this faith in the USA (*Handbook of Denominations*, 1995). But arrogance continued and in 1928 Pope Pius X (1922–1939) declared that only Roman Catholics would enter heaven and extolled the infallibility doctrine. Roman Catholics were forbidden to read or own thousands of books thought to be unfriendly to the faith (the Index Liborium Prohibitorum, first issued in 1559). They must have had also a Movie Prohibitorum for my Catholic friends could not see the movie *Crusades* (Loretta Young and Henry Wilcoxin, 1935) because it showed Catholic kings quarreling. These exalted claims and the micromanagement of thought was a source of contention with many, who had their own religious prejudice, and having an infallible leader had political implications. It was said that as late as 1960 the Catholic presidential candidate, John F. Kennedy, needed church approval for him to enter a Protestant church.

After World War II the Roman Catholic hierarchy changed and in 1962 initiated far-reaching reforms, giving bishops more voice and simplifying church ritual (Vatican Council, 1962–1965*)*. In 1965 they rejected anti-Semitism (CA 3/25/00) and in 1966 abolished the forbidden book idea. And in the 1960s a Catholic priest, Father Vawter, wrote convincingly that we may honor the early religious teaching of the Bible without taking each sentence literally, which denies God's gift of reason, and that the Bible is not a scientific record (*God's Story of Creation*). In 1999 Pope John Paul II, when in Poland, praised the scientific work of Nicholas Copernicus (CA 6/8/99), who 400 years ago showed that the sun did not go around the earth when Scripture said it could stand still and even go backward. The pontiff recently apologized for the treatment of Galileo, for the French Huguenots, and for the many evils committed by many called Roman Catholics— as he put it, "to call good and evil by name" (CA 3/19/00). In India the pope kneeled and prayed at the grave of the renowned Mohandas Gandhi and questioned how the world's largest democracy could have so little religious tolerance (CA 1/6/99). It may be that when Gandhi died, his nonviolence died. As spiritual leader of the world's largest Christian denomination, this pope departed from the hateful piety of the past to give hope for a kindlier and gentler new millennium (CA 3/13/00).

I believe most people also want a gentler, kindlier world. Most religious leaders apparently wish likewise. But vociferous, belligerent religious leaders wish to display their own idea of piety in public, capture headlines, and promote microtheocracy. If you do not agree with them, you are apparently against God, so they imply. They have rallied in Tennessee to demand that the Ten Commandments be displayed in public places to help reclaim America for Christ (CA 1/26/00). Indiana legislators passed just such a law (CA 2/8/00), Mississippi legislators wanted the same (CA 3/3/00), and one Alabama judge posts the Ten Commandments in his courtroom because America's law is based on nature's law and nature is God (3/2/00). The vociferous argue that all laws are traceable to the commandments (CA 4/13/02), but English common law is fundamental in the USA. We have thousands of laws governing taxes, voting, divorce, building, safety, traffic, and the like, but to my knowledge none forces children to honor their parents and have nothing to do with worshipping several gods or graven images, although God is a "jealous God" (Exodus 20:3-5). Vandalism is not mentioned in the Ten Commandments nor is love thy neighbor. In Tennessee, June Griffin persuaded many to post the Commandments illegally in public buildings while refusing to accept a new driver license because the number displayed was "the mark of the beast" (David Waters, CA 4/12/02). A popular mayor of New York City said the Ten Commandments should be posted in the public schools while he broke the one prohibiting adultery (CA 5/10/00). The Bible does not make adultery a lesser crime than murder, only we do. It would be a better world, I believe, if everyone embraced the Ten Commandments (Exodus 21:7-17). But posting these commandments in public ignores the other commandment of Jesus Christ to love thy neighbor as thyself (Matthew 23:39; Mark 13:31, KJV). He said that there was no other greater commandment than this (Mark 13:31). This commandment could be posted as the

Eleventh Commandment by legislators. It might instill respect for others not mentioned in the disputed ten. This eleventh law is also stated in our Old Testament, and the Torah, in Leviticus (19:18); so it could be used more widely to promote respect of one and another. Even the great Chinese philosopher and moralist, Confucius (circa 551– 479 B.C.) had the same idea when he said that we should never do to others what you would not have them do to you. Also, his statement that goodness makes a neighborhood beautiful sounds like a verity (*The World's Great Religions*, Golden Press, 1972). Indeed, when pressed for specifics about which of the commandments would give us eternal life, Jesus lists only six, the last being love thy neighbor (Matthew 19:16-19, KJV).

Also, loving thy neighbor may not be behind the theocratic efforts to teach our Bible in public schools. The Bible history course of Pontotoc County, Mississippi, was deemed by one theologian to be religion, not history (CA 3/6/96). Everything stated in the Bible was fact and no faith was required. According to TV reports, those who opposed the instruction were held in contempt. Some fifteen school systems in Tennessee have Bible courses and the largest wanted to offer Bible history courses, but the State Department of Education disapproved because only the Protestant view was presented (CA 11/18/00). The county Board of Education then considered offering a course in comparative religion, but one adamant board member in opposition proclaimed he was going to protect our children from Hinduism, Buddhism, and voodoo in our schools (CA 11/18/00). Many were appalled, including a Jewish parent and a Buddhist minister. Diversity may be our greatest protection against theocratic politics in the absence of love.

Apparently biblical courses taught in public schools must be constitutional and not be taught as history and be religiously neutral (CA 12/17/00). Florida was chastised for having students ponder such questions as why non-Christians fail to understand some things about God. Should our children learn book, chapter, and verse where God killed people who met with His disapproval but permitted incest? What wars were initiated and helped by God and how many wives did Solomon have? One adamant proponent wants our students to have a true knowledge of the Bible (CA 5/6/00). Most of the letters published in my local newspaper concluded that biblical matters should be left to churches, not government institutions (CA 4/4/00). One writer stated that the county school board would not listen to opposing views and wondered who would teach the courses and whether courses on the Torah, Koran (Qur'an), Veda, and Tipitake might also be offered as an elective. Perhaps school children could learn the religiously neutral facts that Samson slept with a whore (Judges 16:1) and how Amonon raped his sister (2 Samuel 13:14). Instruction in private schools is not limited to religious neutrality so that history may be distorted to serve a religious bias. A colleague once told me his grandchild was taught in an evangelical school that God destroyed the Spanish Armada (1588) with storms to save England from Catholicism—not that the English fleet of fifty-five warships left to Elizabeth I by Henry VIII had a part in the victory. Of course Spain did intend to restore Catholicism—it was another religious war, but by similar reasoning God caused a typhoon in 1274 to destroy the huge fleet of ships sent by the great Mongol ruler Kublai Khan to conquer Japan. The Japanese then called this typhoon the Divine Wind or Kamikaze, not to be confused with the inexperienced Japanese suicide pilots of World War II of that name.

To my knowledge Dante (Dante Alighieri, 1265–1321) was the first to advocate a separation of church and state in his treatise *On Monarchy*. By all accounts he was a devout Catholic and model citizen who lived during the reign of Pope Boniface VII, and later Pope Clement V. Boniface was the last warlike pope of the Middle Ages who insisted on having absolute authority in both civic and spiritual matters. The powerful king of France, Philip the Fair, took issue with the pope over a tax he put on French priests. After Boniface died, Clement V, who was French, moved the papal see (and palace) to France and was subservient to Philip The Fair. Dante detested these corrupt popes and depicted both serving in Hell in his classic work, *Divine Comedy*. Some three hundred years later the clergyman, Roger Williams (1603–1683), founded the colony of Rhode Island and put into practice the idea that church and state must be separate. His biographers say that this separation of church and state became part of our Constitution. In colonial Virginia the Church of England was the legally established form of Christianity and served as an arm of government. The church vestry had the power to tax to pay ministers and custodians, buy land, and build new churches. Legislation imposed fines for religious offenses, like swearing, and if the guilty could not pay they were whipped in public (*Historic Publication of Fredericksburg*, 1981). This power ended with the Revolutionary War and our Constitution. The Quaker William Penn (1643–1718), colonial governor of Pennsylvania with nearly unlimited authority, was a practitioner of religious liberty. The Quakers can rightly claim to have had some of their ideas and ideals incorporated in the U.S. Constitution (*Quaker Influence*, S.B. Hinshaw, 1976). Certainly Benjamin Franklin preferred the freer spiritual atmosphere of Philadelphia to Boston where amusements were prohibited as well as travel on Sunday (*The Private Franklin*, 1975).

David Waters quoted Martin Luther King Jr. in saying that we must live together as brothers or perish together as fools, and pointed out that 5,000 ethnic groups live in 192 nations (CA 9/9/01). This was just two days before the atrocious September 11 attack on New York City and Washington. D.C., against all things American. There are certainly many religious sects: nine for Islam (CA 9/23/01), three Mormon, twenty-seven Baptist, thirteen Methodist, ten Orthodox Catholic, nine Presbyterian, and four for Judaism, among many more (*Handbook of Denominations in the USA*, 1995). Differences in belief and worship routine define each sect and bind members together. Primitive Baptist members wash each other's feet and know that good people will enter heaven even though they never heard of Jesus while members of the huge Southern Baptist Convention don't wash feet but know that salvation is only through Jesus (CA 3/25/00). This large Baptist group (SBC) recently made news by declaring abominable the old Baptist Faith and Message that Christians are each priests with direct access to God and that each have soul competency to interpret the Bible. SBC members heard that soul competency was an acid that destroys authority, that congregations must listen to those that rule, and that the Holy Ghost made one pastor overseer of his church (D. Waters, CA 6/14/00). One leader said, "We will define Scripture for you" (J. Rivera, CA 12/9/00). Southern Baptist agencies must abide to the changes (CA 12/9/00). One Baptist remarked that the changes produce a paper pope (CA *11/5/00)*, and Texas Baptists cut ties with the SBC because it created Baptist popes (CA 10/13/00). The changes also ban women from serving as pastors (CA 12/9/00) which has been open to women since 1845 and where 1,600 have already been ordained (CA 6/4/00). The 5,000 foreign Baptist missionaries had to accept the new dogma or lose funding and face charges of heresy (Alan Breed, CA 6/8/02). Nearly all took the money and changed their articles of faith. The ban was imposed because Paul wrote, "I never let women teach in church or dictate to men" (1 Timothy 2:12). This was a personal (Jewish?) preference as was his suggestion that women should cover their heads in public prayer (I Corinthians 11:5) as Roman Catholics had done but not required to do today. While accepting Paul's personal preference to silence women in church as

65

dogma, SBC leaders ignore his Christian admonition not to do anything that will cause criticism to yourself (Romans 14:16, TLB) and not
to flaunt your faith in front of others who might be hurt by it (Romans
14:22, TLB). Instead, they target Hindus, Jews, and Moslems for con-
version to Christ and officially declare that Hindus are living under the
power of Satan (CA 10/30/99) and false gods (CA 11/7/99). There are
900 million Hindus and many more Moslems and it is strange why the
SBC leaders did not also include some Native Americans
(Amerindians), Shintoists, and many others. At least former president
Jimmy Carter (1976–1980) had heard enough and renounced his SBC
membership in 2000 (CA 10/20/00; CA 10/29/00).

Theocracy requires followers as well as leaders. Too often followers mouth a few words learned from parents or leaders as profound
knowledge of religion and too many leaders proclaim revelations from
above or from sacred writings. Since most humans desire some form
of religion, the unquestioning may be lead by the profane. The relationship may become traditional as in the case of the rattlesnake han-
dlers of Appalachia. The preacher of a Holiness Church died from a
snake bite at the alter of his church just three years after his twenty-
eight-year-old wife died of a similar bite (CA 12/6/98). His last words
included the phrase "God is still God." This snake-handling test of
faith comes from the last verses in the Gospel of Mark where Jesus
purportedly said that true believers can handle snakes or drink any
poison and not be hurt (Mark 16:18). If so, all biblical inerrant dogmatists may consume lethal doses of cyanide, strychnine, or Drano
with impunity if they are true believers. Many scholars question
whether Mark wrote the final verses of that text (Mark 16:19–20) so
that some Bibles contain (KJV, TLB) and one deleted (RSV) these
passages. Nevertheless, some still believe in the correctness of the
snake-handling religion (CA 12/6/98). Likewise, those in India who
destroyed their television sets know their Moslem leader was correct
in declaring that the devastating earthquake of January 26 was due to
immoral TV broadcasts (CA 2/14/01). The followers of Pat Robertson
fund the Christian Coalition who wish to make all things politically
moral while breaking the law concerning political campaigns as a tax-
exempt organization since 1989 (CA 8/7/96). This oversight was corrected, but Robertson still ignores the aforementioned Christian
admonition of Saint Paul and declares as stupid the course of former
Moral Majority leaders to concentrate on evangelism rather than politics (CA 10/9/99). Name-calling is one ugly side of religious dogma-
tism. Franklin Graham arrogantly declared Islam as evil and Pat

Robertson said it was violent. And the Reverend Jerry Falwell put his foot in his mouth again by declaring Islam's prophet Mohammed to be a terrorist (Jacinthia Jones, CA 10/8/02). What the prophet did was help defeat a large army of Arabs bent on destroying his small religious community. The former president of the Southern Baptist Convention, Jerry Vines, also said nasty things about Mohammed and is among those who would support the actions of Israel at any cost only to hasten Armageddon (Tom Teepen, CA 10/19/02). Some have ask why many in Congress, like Tom DeLay of Texas, support the hate speech of the Christian Coalition (CA 10/4/02). The answer is likely to be for votes. Pat Robertson ran unsuccessfully for president in 1980 and in 2002 was satisfied to run Congress. In contrast, Jesus acknowledged that government is secular (Luke 20:25) for his kingdom was not of this world (John 18:36). Religious dogmatists would have it otherwise.

Members of Taliban, currently being attacked by British and U.S. armed forces in Afghanistan for supporting world terrorism (CA 10/16/01), illustrates one consequence of theocracy and that cruelty is the root of evil—although money may be needed. This group reportedly represents the Wahhabi sect of Islam, started in the 1700s, that for one demands severe punishment for enjoying any form of music other than the drum (CA 9/23/01). They have ruled Afghanistan since 1996, destroyed old statues of Buddha as violating a ban on idol worship, closed bath houses for men used mostly by the poor who have not enough water at home, prevent girls older than eight from attending school as well as women from working, and prohibit men from wearing sleeveless shirts, but require them to grow beards (CA 8/13/00). Moreover, Afghan Hindus must wear an identity label, reminiscent of the Nazis who required Jews to wear the yellow Star of David (CA 5/23/01). Even Taliban schoolboys share this religious zeal and shout, "Death to he beardless ones," the Christian missionaries (CA 8/17/00). The militant Sudanese Moslems, the murahaleen, may be even worse. They bomb and bulldoze Christian churches, make all women wear black and veil, rape and make slaves of unbelievers, and plunder. They first exterminated nonmilitant Islamic moderates and since 1983 have killed some 2 million Sudanese (CA 10/25/01). And in Maryland, USA, some Moslem school children are not proud to be an American as their principal explains that our laws and values go counter to the Creator who gave us life (CA 10/25/01). Apparently, there must be no fun in fundamentalism as getting to heaven is serious business. Being civil is unimportant.

The many sects of Islam also illustrate the importance of leaders in the practice of religion. Some of the first followers of Mohammed memorized his revelations from heaven, as well as his political or secular decisions, so that his thoughts could be conveyed to many. The heavenly revelations were eventually written by Zaid ibn Thabit some nineteen years after Mohammed's death and are known as the Quran (Koran). It contains the Ten Commandments, and Noah's Ark, among other basics of Judaism, and declares that Jesus had a miraculous birth and performed miracles but was not divine as there can be but one God. In this regard, Jews and Christians were referred to as people of the book by Mohammed and Moslems are permitted to marry either Jews or Christians. As in our Bible, slavery is permitted but slaves must be treated humanely. In Islamic Sudan slavery is evident (CA 5/23/02) but it occurs in other nations, including the USA, as impoverished people are enticed into bondage (CA 4/2/00; CA 5/17/01). Most of these victims are women and children (CA 6/6/02). However, since slavery is not required, most Islamic nations have outlawed the practice. In addition to the Quran, what the prophet said or did on occasion was eventually put in writing known as Hadiths. These Hadiths are sacred, perhaps like the letters of Paul are to Christians or the Talmud is to Jews. Together, the Quran and Hadiths form the supreme authority on matters of Islam. Sometimes both deal with the same subject such as divorce which is permitted in the Quran while a Hadith says that of all the lawful things divorce is the most hateful to God. But Moslem lives are also governed by religious laws derived from human source that are not specifically covered in the sacred writings. One set of these human laws is called Ijma (consensus) which stems from the Hadith which says Moslems would not agree to error. The other is by Qiyas (analogy) which is based on deductions derived from the sacred writings. For instance, the answer to the question of whether Moslems could eat food prepared by Jews or Christians was yes, within dietary limits, as the Quran permitted marriage to members of those religions. In 114 sura (chapters), the Quran presents a correct version of our Bible and defines the essence of Islam. Moslems must pray five times daily and together on Friday in a Mosque, if possible, and all prayers must be in Arabic. The Moslem twenty-four-hour clock is set at zero at sunset, and during the ninth month of their calendar, Ramadan, they must fast during daylight but may feast all night. In cases of emergency, when fasting is not possible, the days missed are deferred to a later date. Moslems must not consume wine (any alcohol), pork, or blood, although Sura 45 says that wine and the best of fruits will be served by beautiful young women in paradise (heaven). Consumable meats must come from animals whose throats are cut ritualistically, resembling how Orthodox Jews prepare kosher meats.

While the five pillars of Islam are followed by all true Moslems, differences in beliefs and Islamic law, designed to govern everyday life, exist today. The Sunni abhor, for instance, the belief of Shiite Moslems that the brilliant daughter of Mohammed, Fatima, is an instrument of intercession, resembling the prayers to the Virgin Mary by many Catholics. The Quran and Hadiths say nothing about the face veil for women, the custom apparently started in Persia (Iran), but the veil must be worn by law in some nations. Dogs may be used in work but are too unclean to be kept as pets. Profit from the sale of items is approved but profit from the loan of money is forbidden. Whether Moslems can listen to music, wear athletic clothing, own pet dogs, make profit from investments (stocks) and the sale of alcohol, among other characteristics of modern cultures, seems to have a variety of answers by Moslem leaders (J.I. Smith, *Islam in America*, 1999). Parenthetically, our Bible also holds that we must not charge interest from deals we make with our fellow believers (Leviticus 25:36).

Some Moslems argue that the principle of consensus (Ijma) should be used to bring Islamic law (shariah) into harmony with modern conditions. The extraordinary leader Mustafa Kemal Ataturk (1881–1938) solved this dilemma in 1926 as the first president of the Turkish Republic by abolishing Islam as a state religion. In its place the Swiss Civil Code and the Italian Penal Code were adopted (*Encyclopedia Britannica*, 1948). Ataturk started life under an Islamic sultan government, became a superb military leader and statesman, and ultimately turned Turkey into a strong independent democracy, with free public education, where women serve as physicians and even as president. This separation of religion and state is remarkable in that 98 percent of the people are Sunni Moslems while in Saudi Arabia a similar religious population live under their Islamic law. The Moslems of Egypt have much more choice than the Saudis, where a variety of music is heard and women work, even as scientists. The oppression of women in Moslem societies seems contrary to the Quran which affords equal religious merit, and to one of Mohammed's Hadiths which says that all people are equal as the teeth of a comb and states that there is no merit of male over female, white over black, or Arab over non-Arab (John Sbini; *Islam: A Primer*, 1990). The fact that Islamic law is derived from both sacred and human sources has enabled persuasive religious leaders to impose their will on populations, independent of international law. When the repressive regime of the Shah of Iran was ended by revolution in 1979, the Ayatollah Komeini made prisoners of U.S. Embassy staff and ruled the country even more repressively until his death in 1998. Today the judiciary and police of Iran arrest people who own pet dogs (CA 8/26/01) and publicly flog miscreants and close reformist newspapers (CA 8/18/01)

Yet, a large majority elected a reformist, Mohammad Katami, to be their president; and I know that Iranian wrestlers are great sports and enjoyed their recent visit to America. There is hope, yet millions share the sentiments of Osama bin Laden and his ilk, who wish all Americans dead, including 8 million of our Moslem citizens. And many cheered when terrorists killed thousands in New York on September 11. Even many in Kuwait, whose country was raped by Iraq in 1991, sympathize with bin Laden (CA 11/12/01). As of this writing, bin Laden is on the run in Afghanistan, the Taliban has been driven from half of the nation, and by all accounts the remaining Moslems are delighted to see them go (CA 11/18/01). But bullies with enough bullets and money will always have a following as cruelty runs strong in many. Recently in Pakistan Maulana Masood Azhar, surrounded by men brandishing rifles, informed 10,000 cheering followers that Moslems should not rest until India and America are destroyed (CA 1/6/00); and several Algerians, trained in Afghanistan, were caught trying to bomb the Los Angeles airport because Sheik Omar Abdel-Rhman had inspired them (CA 7/9/01). Obviously Moslems differ, but as a group the Wahhabi sect want to return to the life of early Islam—except for modern weapons of destruction. Whether Mohammed would approve of movies, computers, and airplanes is unknown, but he was a reformer and considering his time displayed tolerance toward others. He detested bells, yet David Waters reports he granted a charter of religious freedom to the Christian monks in Mt. Sinai in 628 and declared that Christians are my citizens and by Allah I hold out against anything that displeases them, among other statements of religious tolerance (CA 10/18/01). But today Jews and Christians live in peril in many Moslem communities, and Moslems live in peril among other religious group as well as within different sects of Islam.

The people Tom Brokaw covered in his book *The Greatest Generation* (1998) were not reared to identify America as a Christian nation. They were taught geography, history, arithmetic and the like, but religion was a family affair. They struggled with the great depression and later through WWII holding onto the world view that America was a great place to live and a land of opportunity and hope. They learned that George Washington spent six years away from his home and charged into gunfire to help establish a different kind of nation governed by law—not religion or a king. As president, Washington did everything possible to help establish this great nation. He even personally sold real estate on a cold rainy day in October 1790 to obtain money to finance the construction of Washington. D.C. Congress had given him all authority to build our Federal City without funding the project (*Rider with Destiny—George Washington* by L. Aikman, 1983). Washington was so trustworthy that his subjects let George do it. He was the first to own a mule in America (1785) and invented a better plow. He advocated a national military academy, a free national university, and a national highway system that Congress refused to fund (too much federal power). He also advocated the end of slavery and eventually freed his while slave owners of the Supreme Court, Congress, and many future presidents disagreed. Presidents Jefferson, Madison, Monroe, Jackson, Tyler, Polk, and Taylor continued to own slaves and freed none. Jefferson, always short of money, bred slaves for profit (*Washington—The Man* by J.T. Flexner, 1974). Washington started the celebration of Thanksgiving Day which we still enjoy, but never advocated a national religion.

W.S. Randall documents in his book *George Washington—His Life* (1997) that nearly every conceivable ethnic group (with different religious persuasion) significantly helped establish this nation—Jews, Afro-Americans, English, Italians, French, Scots, Irish, Germans, and Polish, among others. They fought and some went bankrupt to start a radically new way of life, not to start a national religion. Brokaw's Greatest Generation all pledged allegiance to our flag without the phrase "under God," which was added by Congress in 1954. Washington added voluntarily the phrase "so help me God" to the presidential oath of office, but it was not required. With certainty, most of the Greatest Generation did not pray in public schools nor see the Ten Commandments posted in public buildings, but most had a working knowledge of American history and respected our flag (some religious groups do not).

Around 1950 members of our Congress began to modify the First Amendment to the Constitution, perhaps to gain votes or foster patriotism of unborn generations. In 1952 they initiated a National Day of

Prayer, "a government sanctioned day offered to all Americans" (CA 5/3/02). In 1954 by law they added "under God" to our Pledge of Allegiance. In 1956 Congress made "In God We Trust" our new national motto. As David Waters pointed out, these Congressional acts were initiated during election years (CA 5/3/02). In 1988 our prayer day was set for the first Thursday in May, six months before Thanksgiving. Before it had been a "floating holiday." Waters wondered why we need the government to help us pray, and Michael Kelly wondered whether the teaching about the Bible in public schools was not tantamount to waging holy war on the Constitution (CA 5/12/02). Brokaw's Greatest Generation did just fine with secular instruction. They even learned some Shakespeare. In Tennessee they are currently putting up and taking down biblical plaques of the Ten Commandments in public places like courtrooms (Bill Poovey, CA 5/16/02). To some judges the commandments to worship no other God than me (Exodus 20:3, TLB) and not to worship any graven images sounds like religion to them. Those who believe that the promotion of religion is not the business of government have been labeled in recent years as militant secularists by some clergy, especially by televangelists like Pat Robertson and his ilk. Some explain and sell videos showing that this is a Christian nation founded by Christians (but not Quakers) and blame secular historians for hiding the evidence. The advent of television has enabled some to efficiently link religion with government and patriotism, fueled by controversial laws and court decisions. It has also become fashionable to erect huge freestanding crosses for all travelers to see, such as along Interstate 40 near Memphis; Interstate 57 near Effingham, Illinois; and on the water tower of Somerville, Tennessee. Many may welcome this display of faith but it contradicts Paul who advised not to flaunt our faith in front of others (Romans 14:22, TLB) or to keep our faith between ourselves and God (Romans 14:22, RSV), and not to do anything that will cause criticism against us (Romans 14:16, TLB). The last is not always possible but must be a worthy goal set by Paul, our greatest proponent of Christianity. Franklin, Washington, and our other Founding Fathers each lived their own religion and created a new nation based on secular law with the goal of liberty and justice for all. They gave us freedom of religion and from religion being imposed by zealots. Our laws that have evolved to govern traffic, sanitation, child labor, crime, trade, and the like may be objectionable to some and not always perfect, but have served most of us well. Abraham Lincoln in 1863 summarized the nature of our government as one of the people, by the people, and for the people. Our Constitution is more important than any single religion, for without it we might all be subjects of one. History is replete with religious zealots who enjoy being in charge.

The likes of Adolf Hitler (1889–1945) and Joseph Stalin (1879–l953) show that religion is not a requisite for ruthlessness. History also clearly shows that in the name of God militants will impose their religion by force. It is remarkable how such leaders find thousands and millions of ardent followers. While many religious leaders are of that ilk, manifesting disdain for those who do not share their faith, most apparently have as their goal social justice, civility and harmony. The disdainful do not accept religious tolerance, confusing it with immoral permissiveness. Religion, however, without kindness and liberty is tyranny. Theocracy, large or small, has left a dismal record.

CHAPTER 11

Loins and Lies

NEWSPAPERS ARE REPLETE WITH REPORTS OF PEOPLE VIOLATING THE TEN Commandments and the Eleventh to love thy neighbor. Reports of murder, rape, and stealing abound, but the most titillating articles appear to involve fornication, adultery, and lies by individuals of celebrity, power, and trust. While other sins are usually condemned as wrong, it seems today that adultery and lying are most likely to be considered as signs of weakness. The punishment for adultery may be divorce and lying seems harmless except under oath or when used as an instrument to cheat others out of money or property (covetousness).

Alfred C. Kinsey (1894–1956) was an entomologist at Indiana University who felt the need to collect data concerning sexual behavior when told in 1937 to teach a course in sex education and marriage. He and others designed a survey to obtain facts on the subject and found that about 50 percent of the men and 25 percent of women had extramarital affairs, among other findings published in 1948 and 1958. A more recent study showed that infidelity is now far less and attributed the difference to the tumultuous events of World War II where uncertainty, loneliness, and opportunity for indiscretion was great. Nevertheless, I heard the televangelist D. James Kennedy take a different view and said the new report showed that Kinsey and his scientists had lied (presumably to weaken our moral fiber). To lie they would have had to falsify the data and there is no evidence that they did so. Indeed, by all accounts, Kinsey was a good, moral dedicated father of four children (D. Wallechinsky, I. Wallace, *The People's Almanac*, 1975). We should rejoice that there is less infidelity now than fifty years ago, but why didn't the preacher also declare the recent study fraudulent? The absurd statement is often made that there is nothing new under the sun,

74

but the Bible and news reports indicate that there is nothing new in human intercourse. Then as now we have war, cruelty, false preachers, good people, liars, and sexual transgression.

In biblical times we learn that the beloved Ruth was advised not to work alone in a field least she be molested (Ruth 2:22). Sadly we learn that Dinah was raped by Prince Shechem (Genesis 34:2) and that David's son Amnon tricked his beautiful sister into his bedroom to rape her (2 Samuel 13:1–5). He then hated her. Sometimes deception and incest were committed by women. The two daughters of Lot tricked him into having sexual intercourse with him and the children of this incest started two nations (Genesis 19:31–38). Even Abraham married his half-sister and in a cowardly act let King Abimelech take her, declaring she was only his sister (Genesis 20:1–12). Later, Moses made clear that such behavior, and more, was sinful (Leviticus 20:15–21). Nevertheless, David committed adultery with Bathsheba and had her husband killed to cover up the sin (2 Samuel 11). Indeed, adultery was rampant in Jeremiah's time (Jeremiah 7:9; 23:10) and even prophets were guilty of this sin (Jeremiah 23:14). It is unlikely that Jeremiah would dispute the Kinsey Report, but even worse sexual sins were evident during biblical times. While in Sodom, Lot offered hospitality to two male angels and some men surrounded his home and demanded that the angels be raped. Instead, Lot offered his two virgin daughters, but the angels saved the day by bolting the door and temporarily blinding the mob of sex perverts to make their escape (Genesis 19:1–10). One of the most heinous stories in the Bible relates how an old man invited a man and his wife to stay overnight in his home in Gibeah. Again, a mob of sex perverts surrounded the house and demanded that the male guest come out to be raped. Instead, the guest shoved his wife outside where the mob raped her until she died (perhaps of hemorrhagic shock). Not knowing that she was dead, the husband, seeing her at the door, simply told her to get going (Judges 19:21–28, TLB). This dastardly sin soon led to war (Judges 20). The Lord told Moses of many different sexual sins that were punishable by death (Leviticus 20:15–21). This included both parties of adultery (Deuteronomy 22:22). How King David and Bathsheba avoided death by stoning is unexplained. Perhaps the guys who want the Bible to be thoroughly taught to our children in public schools will offer an explanation. That Samson spent one night with a prostitute might be another important fact for children to learn (Judges 16:1).

While stoning of adulterers remains a reality in some Islamic nations, I do not believe orthodox Jews apply this Mosaic law today.

Even Jeremiah did not mention that all those adulterers he knew of were stoned. Jesus was more circumspect on the matter, as he verbally defended a woman from being stoned for adultery (John 8:3–9). He did demand that she sin no more (John 8:11). Indeed, Jesus wanted nothing to do with the incorrigible sinner, all workers of iniquity (Luke 13:27, KJV). Similarly, Paul wrote specifically that a man who cohabits with his father's wife is to be expelled from church membership (1 Corinthians 5:1–2). He further advises us not even to have lunch with those who claim to be Christians but indulge in sexual sins, among other wrongdoing (1 Corinthians 5:9–11). So stoning is out for the Christian, but as Solomon said, one sinner destroys much good (Ecclesiastes 9:18, TLB).

Paul would have probably also agreed with the findings of the Kinsey Report for he recognized that some, like himself, need not marry to avoid sexual sin while for others it was an imperative; as he said, "it is better to marry than to burn with lust" (1 Corinthians 7:6–9, TLB). As with food, where some eat to live while others live to eat, the hunger for coitus reportedly varies. The hunger is best satiated with the help of another warm body. Paul admonishes believers to avoid any sin associated with the hunger but reminds us to expect such sin among unbelievers (1 Corinthians 5:10, TLB). Christians, I believe, consider church members who commit thievery or murder to be by definition unbelievers. In contrast, many seem today to classify lying and adultery as weaknesses, perhaps to be worked on after repentance. As with King David there is usually no repentance unless they are caught by someone like Nathan (2 Samuel 12:1–13).

Among our former presidents, Bill Clinton (1992–2000) is without question the most famous for lying, deception, and adultery. The lying was not only about his adulterous affairs. With a bubbly, magnetic personality he was elected president with about one-fourth of the eligible voters while about one-fourth opposed him. The remaining 50 percent were politically dead. This guy lied about being involved sexually with Gennifer Flowers, Paula Jones, and Monica Lewinsky (Maureen Dowd, CA 1/17/98) and even praised Flowers for lying under oath concerning their long affair (Bob Herbert, CA 2/28/01). The many scandals Clinton and his wife created while in the White House were given special names by reporters, such as Travelgate, Filegate, and Troopergate (David Kushma, CA 2/8/98). The innovative (some say illegal) way he collected political funds is now legendary. He essentially rented rooms in the White House to raise funds and one group of poor American Indians (Native Americans) contributed $150,000 to see the president concerning a land dispute. The leader was given a free meal at the White House, among many other contributors, and was later asked to contribute more money. The tribal members concluded that they had been bilked (CA 3/11/97). His capacity to improvise for select audiences often backfired, with no loss of popularity. While historically only 1 in 20 or 25 (4–5 percent) of all African slaves were exported to the USA (*National Geographic*, Vol. 182, No. 3, 1992), Clinton apologized to the whole world for this cruelty when he was in Africa. The president of Uganda, Yoweri Musveni, said the apology was rubbish for it was the African chiefs who sold their captives for slavery and that they should apologize (Cal Thomas, CA 3/28/98).

When some thirty black and a few white churches were torched in seven southeastern states, Clinton said shortly before his re-election in 1996 that he had vivid and painful memories of black churches being burned in his state when he was a boy (he was born in 1946). Clinton was great at feeling the pain of victims, but the Arkansas NAACP president, Dale Charles, and historians said no black church was burned in Arkansas during his time. Confronted with the fact, the White House was silent (CA 6/10/96). Perhaps the most legally criminal act he performed was during the last minutes of his presidency. Even many (but not all) of his most staunch admirers and sycophants looked askance when he pardoned crimes committed by 176 miscreants. The pardon of the fugitive Marc Rich, who apparently owes 48 million in taxes and illegally bought oil from Iran in 1979, is currently being challenged (CA 12/14/01). The guy who enabled the first lady, Hillary Clinton, to earn $100,000 on a $1,000 investment was pardoned (CA 2/7/01) as were four Hasidic Jews of New York who stole millions from government agencies. That Hasidic group voted for Mrs. Clinton 1,400 to 12 to help her become a senator (Bob Herbert, CA 2/28/01). The questionable actions of Hillary and Bill Clinton are countless, but neither has been jailed, and Bill has been photographed carrying a Bible to church. His talent to obfuscate was perhaps best depicted in a cartoon showing him speaking to the pope. He purportedly said, "Forgive me, Father, for I have spinned" (CA 1/29/99).

Other former presidents known for adultery were Lyndon Johnson (1963–1968), John Kennedy (1960–1963) and Warren Harding (1921–1923). During the impeachment of Clinton (1998), it was often heard that they all do it. The Kinsey Report indicates otherwise and I cannot imagine adultery in the lives of Harry Truman (1945–l953), Herbert Hoover (1929–1933), Theodore Roosevelt (1901–1909), James Garfield (1881), Abraham Lincoln (1861–1865),

James Polk (1845–1849), James Madison (1809–1817), John Adams (1797–1801), and George Washington (1789–1797), among many others. Technically, James Buchanan (1857–1861) never committed adultery because he never married. Even that rascal Thomas Jefferson (1801–1809) was evidently faithful to his beloved wife until she died. Then he used a slave, who was the half-sister to his wife, to satisfy his special hunger.

Members of the Houses of Congress have also provided titillating reading. The Republican Senator (MN) and devout Catholic, David Durenberger, by 1993 had his law license suspended, had many unethical debts, and had had extramarital affairs—one said to have produced a child (CA 4/4/93). In 2001 the charismatic Democratic Congressman Gary Condit acknowledged he had committed adultery, after vehement denials, with Chandra Levy who had mysteriously disappeared (CA 7/13/01). An earlier Gary, Gary Hart, was the darling Democratic candidate for the presidency in 1987 but could not hide his blatant extramarital affair with Donna Rice (CA 7/13/01). A real surprise to me was when in 1974 the powerful Chairman of the Ways and Means Committee, Wilbur Mills of Arkansas, was caught one night in public inebriated with a dancer interestingly named Fannie Foxe (CA 7/13/01). Other notables include Wayne Hays (1976), who paid Elizabeth Ray $14,000 per year to be his mistress; Barney Frank (1990), who liked the prostitute Stephen Gobie; and though not a congressman, Dick Morris, who helped Clinton to be re-elected in 1996 was found living with the prostitute Sherry Rowlands (CA 7/13/01). The Catholic Kennedy clan of Boston has been headliners for Congress over the years. Senator Ted Kennedy reportedly cheated in college, caused the death of a young woman at Chappaquiddick (1969), divorced his wife, staged wild parties, and was instrumental in arranging to have Anita Hill depict our now Supreme Court Justice Clarence Thomas as a sex pervert. Many of us who heard her testimony against Thomas agree with Joseph Perkins who wrote that she had lied (CA 8/25/92). And Representative Joseph Kennedy II divorced his wife Sheila, with whom he had two children, then married Beth Kelly in 1993 and managed to convince the Boston archdiocese to annul the first marriage (CA 5/7/97). Sheila, in turn, wrote a book about the injustice of the annulment (CA 5/7/97). It was said that his plan to become governor of his state was totally destroyed by the book as well as by a contemporary report that his married brother Michael started intimate relations with a fourteen-year-old babysitter that lasted five years (CA 5/7/97). And former Florida Representative Marvin Couch had a perfect record as a member of the Christian Coalition and the God Squad of Congress before he tarnished his image as a family man for hiring prostitutes to service him, one in a shopping center parking lot (CA 3/1/96; 3/2/96). The case of Larry Lawrence suggests that money talks louder than lies for he fabricated a curriculum vitae and a war record, told by him in tears, to become our envoy to Switzerland under President Clinton after giving enough money to the Clinton campaign (CA 12/9/97). After his untimely death, Clinton broke some rules and had Lawrence buried in the Arlington National Cemetery, after which his body was exhumed. One reporter labeled the scandal Gravegate (CA 12/5/97).

The types of individuals who break the seventh and ninth commandments are obviously not limited to politicians. Sometimes they live a secret lie as illustrated by the sad case of Daniel Gajdusek, who won the Novel Prize for medicine in 1976. He was jailed for sexually abusing one of the boys he brought from Micronesia to educate (CA 2/19/97). Pulitzer Prize winners have had their share of liars. In 1981 the journalist Janet Cooke gave up her prize for lying about an eight-year-old heroin addict (CA 4/16/81) and twenty years later another, Joseph Ellis, a professor who won for writing history and who bedazzled students about his combat exploits in Vietnam, lied about serving overseas— never saw Vietnam (CA 8/18/01). Before he was caught whoring, Jimmy Swaggart, cousin of Memphis rock star Jerry Lee Lewis, used to preach to millions as a televangelists and took in 150 million dollars annually. His income must have been more than his cousin Lewis earned and much of it was likely tax-exempt. I once heard him say that Methodist ministers were backsliders and that Mother Teresa (who won the Nobel Peace Prize in 1997) would not go to heaven, to the delight of his audience. Later he preached and played the piano to a smaller audience, but still lives abundantly and condemns Jews and Catholics to hell (CA 12/13/98). While the ordained Baptist minister Jesse Jackson was counseling President Clinton in 1998 on how to politically handle sexual transgression, Jackson was having an extramarital affair with Karen Stanford, who earned $120,000 plus perks, as executive director of his tax-exempt organization (CA 1/19/01; CA 1/22/01; CA 3/6/01). She resigned her position in 1999 to have his baby. One of his supporters excused the affair as human frailty (Cynthia Tucker, CA 1/22/01). Perhaps Clinton's example led him astray.

The Amish dress simply for their religion, but some act like wolves in sheep clothing. Recently two Amish men were sent to prison for selling cocaine to Amish youths (CA 7/1/99), and one licentious old Amish male appeared in court charged with raping two girls and gross sexual imposition. He later pleaded guilty of five counts of sexual battery instead of eleven charges. An Amish bishop would have preferred to punish him by shunning and avoid secular courts completely (CA 10/31/01). The Church of Jehovah Witnesses is another closed society that one member criticized for avoiding secular authority in cases of child abuse among its members (CA 5/10/02). Shunning does occur within families. Joe and Barbara Anderson were devoted Jehovah members for forty years but were made outcasts when they openly objected to how Witness elders kept secret cases of child molestation committed by fellow church members. Their complaint reportedly caused some church members to defect when aired on NBC's *Dateline*. Their son declared that they would never see him or their grandson again because the defectors will die at Armageddon (CA 9/26/02). His religious motto seems to be: Remember the Armageddon, forgive child molesters, and forget devoted parents. One leading Mormon moralist, who spent years denouncing sexual abuse of children, tearfully apologized for coercing a fourteen-year-old girl to perform sexual acts behind a radio station in Salt Lake City (CA 1/23/96), and one rabbi stated that his promiscuous sex life was wrong, but denied he murdered his wife (CA 10/31/01). A Hasidic rabbi tried his best to molest a girl while on a flight from Australia (CA 6/3/95) and a different kind of rabbi was arrested for soliciting sex with a male teenager (CA 4/8/01). In Israel the sentence of former defense minister Yitzhak Mordechai for raping two female subordinates was suspended because of his valuable service to the government (CA5/l/01) and a mayor of San Francisco, Willie Brown, rejoiced that he fathered a baby out of wedlock (CA 4/11/01).

So much religious literature is published in Tennessee that the state might be considered the Bible Belt buckle, USA. But some ministers have sinfully let down their pants and their followers. Nashville is the home of the publishing house for the National Baptist Convention of America whose membership is said to be 8.5 million strong. Their former convention president, Reverend Henry Lyons, is currently in prison for racketeering and grand theft involving church funds. Lyons claims $7.8 million in debts (about ninety-two cents per church member) and might still be free if his wife had not torched the home he bought for another woman. The arson triggered an investigation of his financial dealings (CA 9/17/97; CA 4/7/01). By comparison, the Nashville Church of Christ minister David Slater, who had been a country and gospel singer, was a piker for he was jailed only for breaking into cars and forgery (CA 7/11/01). Another Tennessee minister, while married, shot the man he caught in bed with the woman he had been having an affair. The judge in charge thought it was a tough case (CA 5/10/01). A simpler case, apparently, was that of Reverend Joseph Combs of Bristol, Tennessee. He was sentenced to jail for 114 years for kidnapping a girl from an orphanage in 1978 that he reared to rape, abuse, and serve as slave. His wife only received a fifty-five-year sentence for her part (CA 4/26/00). In another Bible state, Texas, the board chairman of Southwest Baptist Theological Seminary resigned in 1998 because he was physically intimate with two women he was counseling (CA 10/7/98).

Roman Catholic history has been tarnished by clerics who ignored their holy vow of celibacy. Early in the Tudor era, the Catholic Church of England could inflict penalties on laymen for numerous offenses. The fine for having an illegitimate child was two pounds, but clerics who begot a bastard only paid five shillings, the money going to the church. On the other hand, the bastard son of Cardinal Wolsey (who had built the great palace of Hampton Court) held thirteen ecclesiastical offices while still a schoolboy (Christopher Morris, *The Tudors*, Collins Press, 1968). The history of the papacy that covers nearly sixty years (A.D. 904–963) has been called The Rule of Harlots (*Halley's Bible Handbook*, 1965). It started with Sergius III who was elected pope in 898, the same year as Pope John IX, but John was strong enough to have Sergius expelled from Rome. Sergius reappeared in 904, had the papal claimants Leo V and Christopher strangled, and became pope (*Encyclopedia Britannica*, 1948). Sergius reportedly had a son by Marozia, the daughter of the powerful couple who made him pope. The son later became a pope. When Sergius died, the mother of Marozia, Theodora, arranged to make Anastasius (911–913), Lando (913–914), and John X (914–928) popes, it is said, to gratify her passions. Then Marozia took over, arranged the death of John X in 928, and raised to the papacy Leo VI, Stephen VII, and then her illegitimate son, John XI (931–936). Later a grandson of Marozia became Pope John XII (955–963). John was a political rascal and Otto the Great of Germany forced him to leave Rome and installed Leo VIII as pope. But when Otto left Rome, Leo also left when John returned. Pope John XII was a rascal with women: violating virgins and widows alike, and living with the mistress of his father. He was murdered in 963 while in the act of adultery by the husband of the woman. The people immediately elected Benedict V as pope but Otto returned to Rome that same year and again made Leo pope (963–965). Father Filippo Tamburini used Vatican documents without permission to write *Saints and Sinners*. It tells of a nun who killed her two children, of forgery, castration, and many other sins committed by monks, priests, and nuns some five hundred years ago. The book reportedly sold like hotcakes and was in a second printing (CA 3/17/95). Only the lurid parts of the book made headlines in Italy.

In our time, Pope John Paul II has acknowledged that some Catholic officials have done dastardly deeds. In Ireland, officials of the Catholic order of Christian Brothers have publicly apologized for members who have sexually abused children in their care (CA 3/29/98), and the pope met with Irish bishops to deal with many pedophile scandals involving clergy in their country (CA 6/27/99). The Catholic Diocese of Dallas, Texas, paid $19 million to the boys abused by a priest between 1981 and 1992 (CA3/29/98) while the Catholic Diocese of Nashville, Tennessee, was sued by two boys for $70 million who were abused by a priest (CA 8/26/00). In California a dozen priests were found to have abused thirty-four teenage boys (CA 11/30/93), and in Massachusetts a Catholic youth leader responded guilty to charges that he molested twenty-nine children (CA 7/10/01). One happy-looking Swiss bishop resigned his office after he admitted fathering a child, and it was reported that he was the fourth Catholic bishop to resign within five years for having affairs with women (CA 6/3/95). Some priests use nuns to satisfy their special need, particularly in Africa where some priests consider celibacy to mean unmarried, and who wish to avoid AIDS (CA 3/21/01). One report to the Vatican indicated that priests and bishops have committed sexual crimes in twenty-three countries (CA 11/23/01) and another that the Holy See will try priests accused to being pedophiles (CA 1/19/02). Apparently in the past errant priests were sent from diocese to diocese and their misdeeds hushed, but this pope seems to wish to deal with the problem. Among other things, it is costing the church money. To my knowledge, however, the many priests (and nuns) who served my friends and family members for some seventy-five years have all been most honorable.

Someone said that success is sexy. It must be so for many fervently follow successful athletes, politicians, musicians, and movie stars, among others. A line in an old song was that "you have to be a football hero to get along with the beautiful girls." Frank Sinatra was not into football, and not especially handsome, but as a great entertainer got married four times and was friends of gangsters and politicians alike. Despite his many divorces, a special mass was conducted by Cardinal Roger Mahony to honor his life when he died in 1998 (CA 5/17/98). Kirk Douglas was an undefeated college wrestler and superb actor who wrote a candid autobiography (*The Ragman's Son*, 1988). He tells of intimate wrestling affairs with actresses Marlene Dietrich, Joan Crawford, Evelyn Keys, and Gene Tierney as well as with many, many other women. Lucky for him science had under control the older venereal diseases and AIDS had not become prominent until he had settled down. The splendid actors Katharine Hepburn and Spencer Tracy carried on a long adulterous affair that became public after his death. Later Hepburn said that Tracy could not divorce his wife because he was Catholic. His stance may not have been so honorable, for Douglas reveals that Tracy once tried to date Gene Tierney. Errol Flynn, the quintessential movie hero, was said to be carnal with 10,000 women. If so, it does not speak well of womanhood. Clark Gable was apparently far less promiscuous than many, but he did father a child with Loretta Young who was Catholic. While eroticism is associated with the entertainment business, the likes of Bob Hope, Danny Thomas, Bing Crosby, and Maureen O'Sullivan suggest that promiscuity is not a requisite to happiness or success.

Others have said that power is the ultimate aphrodisiac. In Cuba the all-powerful Fidel Castro reportedly begot illegitimate children and at seventy declared that he loves women (CA 3/24/97). As Reich Minister for Propaganda, Dr. Joseph Goebbels (1887–1945) used his power so excessively to compromise women that his wife wanted a divorce. Instead, Joseph was duly chastised by his boss Adolf Hitler (H-O Meissner, *Magda Goebbels*, 1980). In his propaganda, however, Goebbels would condemn Jews for their lechery. The military is built on power of authority and some male superiors may take advantage of their charge (CA 6/27/99), and sometimes female recruits have consensual sex with superiors and claim rape, lying about fornicating (CA 3/11/97). Success in sports, business, or just having money or a title makes some sexually attracted to others, particularly women to men. But men mainly support the so-called oldest profession (prostitution) that ranks in profit only third to the sale of illicit drugs and arms (CA 7/28/00).

Socrates once explained the attraction of the sexes. He said that male and female were originally one body, with two heads, four arms and so forth. This combination made for so much happiness that it irritated the gods. In their anger they divided the creature and humans have been trying to get together ever since. One effective televangelist (JH) defined sex as being a hormonal driven urge to merge.

Ann Landers referred to it as one pair of glands talking to another pair. Whatever it is, it is biological rather than spiritual. Civilized humans, however, have greater choices than other animals. We may or may not, more or less, have children and rear them under cultural restraints. Biologists can pretty well tell us how adult animals will behave: the male penguin will take care of the eggs till they hatch while the male lion will take care of himself. Although many other animals learn new behavior, the behavior of the human is most diverse, be they farmers, cab drivers, detectives, naturalists, musicians, or physicists. Many animals are faster and stronger, but no other single species can match the diverse physical capabilities of humans. This becomes evident when we watch the many movements of the gymnast, the different strokes of the swimmer, the complex maneuvers seen in football or ballroom dancing, and realize that at least some can outrun a horse. The genius of a few have even enabled us to fly. And we seem to be the only species on earth that ponders whether there is a soul. Gerald Schroeder states that man is the only animal that has a soul, *neshama* in Hebrew (*The Science of God*, 1997). His proof, however, comes from Scripture. Nevertheless, we appear special in spending time, energy, and/or money to capture a sense of spirituality that stems from pondering the unknown. Spirituality is not limited to religion as exemplified by the astronomer David Levy who wrote "a darkening sky and a starry night never cease to fill me with wonder, a feeling of awe shared with diverse individuals who have watched the sky over thousands of years" (*Parade* section, CA 12/23/01). Lechery is not spirituality. No wonder that in his ministry evangelist Billy Graham did not travel, meet, or eat alone with any woman but his wife to avoid any suspicion of impropriety (Terry Mattingly, CA 10/9/99).

While pious miscreants obviously abound, it is also apparent that many reap rewards from religion without ruining the lives of others. Religion can bring dignity, joy, and comfort through baptisms, weddings, funerals, and special group activities. The young can learn social skills in religious classes, first communions, and bar mitzvahs. They can learn to be civil and about obligations and punctuality. Adults may be channeled to help those in need and contribute to the practical lessons taught to members of the Boy and Girl Scouts. At sites of worship people have special places to assemble and support each other in times of calamity. Religion has changed many lives for the better. One neighbor we knew had had a miserable childhood, left home at age sixteen, married, joined a supportive Baptist church with her husband after hearing Billy Graham preach, taught Sunday school, learned to like learning, earned her GED, and reared a fine family. Her religion did not prevent her need to be treated for cancer but helped her to endure. Her church affiliation, arguably, may have only strengthened her propensity for goodness, but it was available and it worked.

CHAPTER 12

Logic, Spirits, and Modernism

WILL DURANT STATES THAT ZENO WAS THE FATHER OF LOGIC BUT CREDITS Aristotle with formalizing the topic with the introduction of deductive reasoning that he called syllogism, and with inductive reasoning: the foundation of science where from facts theories are born (*The Life of Greece*, 1939). Aristotle's textbook of logic was used by scholars for two thousand years after his death in 322 B.C. Thus many texts report him to be the father of logic. Aristotle defined things with words, such as man is a rational animal. He criticized his predecessors for creating theories out of their heads "instead of devoting themselves to patient observation and experiment." The essence of his formal logic was that facts or statements must not be contradictory if theories or conclusions are to be valid. We, however, often use logic to simply mean that the evidence or statements support our position. How problems are solved is often mysterious. The answers to problems have occurred to some after sleep or during unguarded moments as while taking a bath, a phenomenon psychologists call incubation. Insight is another mystery. Here an answer may suddenly appear after pondering a problem for some length of time, independent of syllogism or induction. It is also mysterious how countless fashions, sports, mores, medical remedies, songs, superstitions, and religious practices have come from someone's head. None of the social animals that have been studied manifest the array of behaviors of humans, nor inhabit such a variety of shelters, from igloo to castle. The early progress man made from the cave era was the result of accident, coincidence, trial and error, and the ingenuity to adapt new findings to social needs, largely by the use of our complex languages. What is called modern, however, exists only because of science and its close partner engineering. Arguably

86

man is a rational animal, but modern life rests on the work of rare geniuses like James Clerk Maxwell (1831–1879) and Charles Proteus Steinmetz (1865–1923), the scientist-engineer. It is rare because what the likes of Tesla did, millions could not. While most trained in science will not make epic discoveries, those educated in the sciences can better support and even take advantage of novel findings. As a boy I read that only twelve scientists could evaluate the mathematical theories of Albert Einstein (1879–1955). I often wondered why the number was an even dozen, and who counted, but by now the number must be higher. Likewise, many today use the calculus developed centuries ago by the geniuses Isaac Newton (1642–1727) and Gottfried Wilhem Leibnitz (1646–1716). Indeed, today science is requisite to many professions and those identified as scientists are requisite to modern life, serving in many capacities. Objectivity and reality are inherently part of the study of science, and science teachers can impart to students its importance to life and introduce them to a rigorous way of thinking. We often hear the news that scientists are investigating a problem, such as the source of anthrax or the cause of Ebola. That implies that facts will rule the day. From facts logical conclusions may be drawn by induction. When conclusions drawn by humans are contradictory, we suspect something is wrong. When the behaviors of people contradict their pronouncements, we suspect something is wrong. Logic has not, however, played a role in the development of the great variety of religious beliefs and forms of government of today and throughout history. Even some trained in the sciences, including logic, have been known to act foolishly. Police reports alone indicate how irrational man may be and suggest that Aristotle's definition has limits. We have been scientifically classified as being *Homo sapiens*, the later half meaning intelligent. One zoology professor thought that went too far and said it should be "Homo sap-eons."

Ralph Waldo Gerard, M.D., Ph.D., was a prominent scientist who I knew casually but admired. He developed the capillary microelectrode to study single neurons, had a profound understanding of brain function, and helped create the new campus of the University of California at Irvine, initiating a strong program in computer science in the late 1960s. He learned to be curious at an early age from his father who was an engineer. Gerard was a superb lecturer and liked to emphasize that the methods of science gave the findings validity. Indeed Harold E. Himwich, M.D., who discovered in 1929 that the brain used only glucose for fuel, went so far as to tell us that new methods create new sciences. This seems self-evident, but emphasizes the dependency of science on inventiveness and the development of new technologies. Prior to WWII I believe more teachers and students were conversant with the scientific method than today, in part because more time was spent on the history leading to new discoveries, more teachers learned the philosophy of science somewhere, and the science curriculum was broader. In those days college biology majors commonly took physics, chemistry, some math, biology, botany, zoology, histology, bacteriology (now called microbiology), human physiology/anatomy, psychology, biochemistry, often physical chemistry, embryology, and comparative anatomy. Medical schools also required applicants to have had embryology and comparative anatomy for admission, both subjects where evolution was likely to be perceived. By 1960 the medical schools I knew dropped those subjects for admission and many colleges modernized their science curriculum. Several years ago I met a woman who held a bachelors degree in biology that had never heard of comparative anatomy (her biology was mainly biochemistry) and I know a scientist who obtained a Ph.D. in physiology who never studied the subject. He had no idea what factors regulate blood pressure nor how the brain worked, for example. His specialty was the new, dynamic field of molecular biology. I know of a botanical geneticist who was told to teach pharmacy students about drugs. He never had a course in the subject and no history of an interest, so he taught unsuccessfully. The pharmacy dean removed him as a teacher. I have heard from college students, my granddaughter included, who have had math teachers that could not teach because their English was unintelligible. Students withdrew from class or ended up with poor grades or worse. It is fraudulent to offer such courses to students. It has no teacher and has no course. The recent advances in science have blurred the academic scene, especially in medical schools. For example, in the old days a leading anatomist may have studied the structural changes associated with trauma but today may wish to find out what genes are involved in tissue repair. He may hire a talented molecular biologist to help find the answer and arrange a permanent appointment to give him security. The anatomy department then has a faculty member ignorant of comparative anatomy, embryology, gross anatomy, neuroanatomy, and the like. New chairmen hired from another institution typically bring their own research staff, many with no knowledge of the discipline they represent. I worked for five chairmen and, with one exception, each knew they knew better than the last. New curricula have also blurred the lines between some traditional disciplines. One new dean of medicine, Al Farmer, at my university was a chain smoker who knew a better way to learn basic medical science. He and his cronies forced medical students to learn gross anatomy with plastic models and homogenized the first two years of the curriculum into a systems type. The students were to learn better ways to think and use self-discovery to solve medical problems. The students and their clinical teachers finally revolted and after four years the old, traditional curriculum was reinstated. The dean was not fired, continued to smoke, took a job elsewhere, and died of a heart attack at age fifty-two. He was not the first, nor will be the last, to leave the classroom to become a flawed educator. Even Harvard and Yale Universities have unsuccessfully tampered with their medical curricula (*Science* 181:1027–1032, 1973).

There is nothing sacred, however, about traditional education and some changes are obvious, like the introduction of computer science. Indeed, the likes of computer science, marine biology, ecology, and bioengineering compete with and alter the traditional science curriculum. It is sad, however, when some have the power to change a curriculum affecting hundreds to millions (remember the new math?) because they declare, without proof, that it is a superior way for all students to learn. One of the great teachers of Ralph Gerard, Ajax Carlson, of the University of Chicago often asked students and colleagues alike, "What is the evidence?" I am sure that he would have asked the same of the innovative educator. But today evidence is irrelevant to many educators, for everyone is entitled to their opinion. Gerard was a brilliant student who earned a Ph.D. at age twenty-one and who had a "devotion to reason as a way of life." He exemplified Aristotle's definition of mankind. Gerard died in 1974 at age seventy-four (*The Neurosciences: Paths of Discovery*, eds.: Wordens, Swazey, Adelman, 1975).

Stanley Cobb was a well-known Harvard neuropathologist who wrote books like *Foundations of Neuropsychiatry* (1952). As a sideline he tried to identify a common trait among his colleagues that might explain their success. He found none, but most did attend universities that attract bright students. In this regard, Gerard stated that he learned much from his students and repeats the story about Harvard being a repository of knowledge because freshmen enter with great knowledge and graduate knowing so little. In the aforementioned book, Cobb notes that great men of science varied tremendously in energy and in size, from the massiveness of R. Jung to the leanness of E.D. Adrian. He also noted that most of the sixty men chosen to receive honorary degrees during Harvard's tercentenary celebration had bright eyes, good minds (of course), and boundless energy. It is, however, clear that the intelligence necessary to work in science is independent of personality—some are modest, some arrogant, some sedentary, some athletic, and so forth. We are told that the behavior of the alpha male wolf is fairly well defined, but the personalities of successful academics, physicians, lawyers, architects, and engineers, among others, vary tremendously. And the ability to teach is independent of Intelligence Quotients. Max Planck in his *Scientific Autobiography* (1949) describes the terrible teaching of the great scientist Hermann von Helmholtz while he lauds the teaching of his high school math teacher, Hermann Muller. I once read a report that concluded, in bold print, that doing much scientific research does not enhance the ability to teach. I believe the conclusion was valid, but the report also showed that those who did research taught as well or as poorly as those who did not. No one could conclude from the report that less research meant better teaching, as the boldly stated conclusion had implied.

Another curiosity is why the highly educated act so contrary to reason. Alfred North Whitehead (1861–1947) was evidently beloved by all and with Bertrand Russel wrote the classic on mathematical logic *Principia Mathematica*. This preeminent proponent of logic would, however, periodically purchase items far in excess to his ability to pay. His wife, who paid all bills, would not confront him with the problem because Whitehead had an insane fear of debt. Russel secretly paid the bills and told no one about the insanity until after Whitehead died (*The Autobiography of Bertrand Russel*, 1961). The great early neurologist J.H. Jackson (1835–1911) had a different insanity. He would tear select pages from books he borrowed (*John Hughlings Jackson—Father of English Neurology*, Oxford Press, 1998). Gail Parker left a professorship at Harvard to become the youngest woman college president of Bennington, Vermont, in 1972. She apparently offended nearly everyone, openly committed adultery, and was accused of making educational policy in the bedroom. She lasted four years, married the adulterer, and became a lobbyist (*Newsweek*, May 26, 1980). The title "best academic tyrant" seems to go to John Silber (Ph.D. in philosophy), a president of Boston University. The faculty voted 475 to 215 to oust him, clerical workers went on strike, and they had four labor strikes under his learned guidance. He called his opponents morons and said his job was like a rabbit making love to a skunk and "I enjoy it as much as I can stand." But finances improved and Boston University got a winning football team (CA

5/25/80). Finances seemed great at Stanford University partly because their president Donald Kennedy used federal dollars to pay for an antique fruitwood commode, for flowers for a horse stable celebration, renovations of the college yacht, and for his wedding reception to improve faculty morale. Some $200 million to Stanford to support research was in question, perhaps due to faulty accounting (CA 3/18/91). Dr. J. Wade Gilley became president of the University of Tennessee system in 1999 and resigned about a year later for health reasons, after wooing and promoting a younger female faculty member. When plans to redo the quadrangle of my university surfaced around 1994, the plea of the gardener to add a sprinkler system was ignored. It took bulldozers, a huge crane, many workers, and over half million dollars to make the quadrangle look about how it did before. But now after a rain, puddles of water impede human traffic and in the heat of summer water hoses do likewise. About thirty years ago my boss made an inane comment to a university electrician concerning an old inoperative window air conditioner. Later the electrician was overheard saying to another worker "sometimes yah gotta wonder how smart people think." At least sometimes they don't.

Despite the fact that academics too often manifest aberrant behavior, to my knowledge most have kept in touch with reality. Those into science, mechanics, engineering, surgery, and the like must be in touch with reality or fail. Policemen, firemen, and those in the armed services must face reality or fail. Even the art of dance and sports are limited by reality. But with fiction men may become invisible, invincible, live among dinosaurs, and fly on the backs of geese. Flash Gordon dealt with lion men and hawk men who flew while Tarzan killed gorillas and lions without obvious injury. Stories like *Snow White and the Seven Dwarfs* and *Lord of the Rings* have captivated millions. While many adults draw a line between reality and fiction, some remain as small children who cannot.

The desire to believe in the unbelievable is strong in some. Sir Arthur Conan Doyle, the author of Sherlock Holmes stories, is a case of point. Doyle was trained to be a physician at Edinburgh University and was knighted by King Edward VII (1901–1910) for his practical service during the Boar War (1899–1902). Doyle maintained that we could communicate with the dead via séances even after Harry Houdini and others proved the practice fraudulent. Doyle admitted that some "spiritualists" were frauds but knew some were genuine. He was not alone; the scientist William Crookes and the famed psychologist philosopher William James were among a group who did psychical research. The physicist Oliver Lodge knew one spiritualist who brought back from the dead the spirit of his beloved aunt. Doyle insisted that one photograph showing several fairies with young girls was real even after the girls declared it a hoax when they got older. Americans were not immune to spirits. Doyle lectured at Carnegie Hall and afterward police reported many suicides by people who were eager to get to the next world. One woman murdered her two-year-old, drank a bottle of Lysol, and slowly died expecting to meet her husband in the other world. In contrast, the mother of Doyle thought it was all nonsense (Chas. Higham, *The Adventures of Conan Doyle*, 1976). Spiritualism and ectoplasm are no longer fashionable, but mental telepathy, near death experiences, new age religion, new age psychics (modern fortune tellers), hearing directly from God, miracles, and guardian angels make the news. Indeed, Wendy Kaminer reports how Della Reese, who plays the role of an angel on the TV show "Touched by an Angel," was told directly and clearly by God to do the show as a favor to Him. The idea of telekinesis is that we can move objects by thought. The ability to do so has been, of course, shown to be fraudulent, but Kaminer reports that Kevin Ryerson tells his followers that through thought we can turn on and off DNA. This is surely the first report of biochemical telekinesis. Thomas Edison believed in psychokinesis and thought that with the right electronic device we could communicate with the dead (W. Kaminer, *Sleeping with Extraterrestrials*, 1999). During his time many thought electricity had curative properties. After all, it did wonders for Frankenstein's monster. I heard a debate in 1968 by two professors concerning the evidence for mental telepathy and premonition at an English university. An old retired professor vigorously presented his positive evidence while the other did his best to refute the evidence. A university student was the moderator and at the end of the debate asked for all those in the audience to raise their hands if their minds were changed on the subject. He was warmly applauded for this adroit diplomacy.

Someone said that you cannot maintain religious values without ritual. That axiom obviously applies to billions of people. To the axiom may be added symbols like the crescent, the cross, the star, and the icon of Eastern Christians. Statues may be important as with Hindus, Catholics, and Buddhists. Chanting may be used as with Catholic and Buddhist monks and Hindus. Hindus and Catholics (on Ash Wednesday) may use forehead markings. Some may have beads as Moslems (for the ninety-nine names of God) or as Catholics with the Holy Rosary. They may remove shoes before entering places of worship, as do Moslems and Hindus. They may wash hands before praying as with Moslems and Shintoists or use water in different ways for Christian baptism. Christians may line up for Holy Communion to drink some wine (or grape juice) with bread. Men and/or women may dress special as in the case of the Amish, Orthodox Jew, Moslem, Sikh, and Hindu, and men may grow beards. A meteorite may be designated sacred as with the Moslems and several Native American tribes of Oregon (CA 2/19/00). Worshippers may light candles, wash feet and, as with Zoroastrians, fire may be important religiously. Some may handle poisonous snakes, and many sing and play music. Many kneel and/or bow their heads in prayer. Some religious rituals add luster to special events, like the Church of England rites of coronation for Elizabeth II in 1952 and the Shintoism displayed during Sumo wrestling tournaments of today. Many early Christians paid homage and paid to see religious relics. At Walsingham, England, they saw a bottle containing milk of the Virgin Mary, and at Canterbury the bones of Saint Thomas with some flesh attached that was still bleeding (Christofer Morris, *The Tudors* 1968). The renowned English Catholic martyr, author of *Utopia*, Sir Thomas More, was a staunch believer in relics and in punishing heretics with torture in the basement of his home (CA 3/31/85). On television we may see religious relics still used to prevent disasters and Peruvian Christians paying homage to a sacred mountain. Many Christians visit Fatima, Portugal, for miracles; millions of Moslems travel each year to Mecca; and for Kumbh Mela, 65 million Hindus wash their sins away every twelve years in the Ganges River (CA 1/10/01). Amongst this caldron of religious fervor logic and science plays no role. And most of the 6 billion people on earth don't mind.

Most religious leaders likewise don't give a mind to logic or science. In the extreme case, only religion may be taught. In Pakistan, President Pervez Musharraf on January 12, 2002, vowed to reform the Islamic schools that taught only the Quran and militancy, that was part of a political mosque-military alliance established by the former dictator General Zia (CA 1/25/02). Earlier, some mullahs (religious teachers) like Sufi Mohammed of Pakistan gave weapons to untrained youths and sent them to fight for the Taliban forces in Afghanistan to die, even after veteran soldiers pleaded with him not to. Of the sixty youths sent, only twenty-five returned and they were surprised that the only opposing soldiers they saw were Moslems. Many locals criticized the mullah and he was arrested for possessing illegal weapons (CA 12/4/01). The most famous recent mullah is Mohammed Omar, former spiritual leader of Afghanistan and of the Taliban government starting in 1996. Under his dynamic leadership music, television, kite flying, photography, or painting was forbidden and all images of people or animals were destroyed, including ancient statues of the Buddha. Women were forced to be covered from head to over foot by means of the awkward burqas (CA 12/7/01). He welcomed Osama bin Laden, his money, and other Arabs to strengthen his regime of 24 million people (CA 12/13/01). In turn bin Laden was free to school terrorists who apparently attacked New York City and the Pentagon on September 11, 2001. Their goal was not to help the poor or repair the infrastructure of their country, nor teach science.

We also have many, many Christian leaders in our country who reject logic and science, declaring the Bible is flawless to the applause of millions. When the Southern Baptist leader W.A. Criswell died at ninety-two years of age, a news heading read that he never wavered on inerrancy of the Bible (CA 1/11/02). I heard him interviewed once on TV, I believe by Bill Moyers, and Criswell said that Scripture was accurate in all things—historically and scientifically. This means that astronomers should teach that the sun may stand still (Joshua 10:13) or go backwards (Isaiah 38:8), zoologists must teach the lion is the strongest (king) of beasts (Proverbs 30:30, KJV), ignoring the elephant or rhinoceros, and that an ass (donkey) spoke to the magician Balaam (Numbers 22:28-30, KJV). Must geologists declare that the Jordan river was made by God to keep people apart (Joshua 22:24–25, TLB) and botanists teach that olive trees and other plants may speak to man and converse with each other (Judges 9:7–15)? Then historians must teach that Noah was the first to circumnavigate the earth. Secular scholars tell us that Ferdinand Magellan was killed by unfriendly Phillipino natives in 1521 and that Del Cano then piloted Magellan's crew to be the first to go around the world. But the Bible story is most certainly older than 1521. Noah and his family not only circumnavigated the earth but collected animals along the way as revealed in the chapter "Genesis and Zoology." And he did it without motors or sails. Creation scientists might find and display the great fish (it was not a whale) that swallowed Jonah and explain to the world how Jonah lived somewhere inside under water for three days (Jonah 1:17). That would be creative. The inerrant biblical biochemist may also teach how we humans started out as dust from the ground (Genesis 2:7) but now make proteins and DNA. Even the scientific explanations of Genesis espoused by the religious creation scientists are flat wrong because the Bible told the story first and accurately, according to the biblical inerrant dogmatists.

Why the biblical inerrant dogmatist has embraced creation science defies logic. The creation scientist does not believe in the inerrancy of the Bible as discussed previously in "Evil Evolution." But both groups demonize what they call the scientific establishment, especially astrophysicists and anyone connected with studies using the prefix *paleo*. The scientific establishment is affiliated with universities in cities like Tokyo, Kyoto, Beijing, Delhi, Moscow, Cracow, Warsaw, Ankara, Rome, Paris, Berlin, Heidelberg, Stockholm, London, Cambridge, Edinburgh, Dublin, Cairo, Sofia, Johannesburg, Sao Paulo, Sidney, Boston, Chicago, Los Angeles, Montreal, and countless other cities. They are also located in many museums and research institutes. In the past 150 years or so, many establishment scientists have independently collected data in astronomy, geology, and biology that reflect on early events on our earth and universe. That data has been examined by thousands of other independent scientists. Their conclusion regarding the history of life and age of the earth appalled the biblical inerrant dogmatists who declared the conclusions fraudulent. The handful of creation scientists tell us that the conclusions were simply based on questionable instrumentation, faulty interpretation of the data and state that dinosaurs and man co-existed. Also, everything that is or has been on earth is no more than 10,000 years old. If so, then any notion that there have been periodic ice ages going back 25,000 to a million years is bunk and the recent map in National Geographic (December 2001) showing the fossil Cryolophosauris that lived in Antarctica some 200 million years ago, when the continent was warmer, is also bunk. Academic scientists have reported that an enormous lizard (ichthyosaurs) swam earth's ancient oceans and became extinct about 90 million years ago (*Science News*, 8/24/02) but creationists debunk such data for they know that living creatures first appeared on earth only several thousand years ago. To fight the evil influence of academic or secular scientists, the biblical inerrancy dogmatists are building creation museums, the most recent in Kentucky lead by Ken Ham (CA 12/16/01). Here children can see for themselves Adam and Eve living blissfully alongside Tyrannosaurus rex in Eden. Moreover, they all sprang to life on day six of creation. Ham is not deterred by criticism for, he says, "This is a cultural war." They may have won already for in one poll 68 percent of Americans favored teaching creationism in public schools and 45 percent agree we came from dust less than 10,000 years ago. Moreover, Nicholas Kristof wrote that a recent Gallup poll showed that 48 percent of Americans believe in creationism while only 28 percent are with evolution, and that our president, G.W. Bush, rejects the science of evolution (CA 3/6/03). Ham has also targeted errant Christians for not taking every word in the Bible as fact. If so, we know that an olive tree did talk to a grape vine and that Noah was the first to circumnavigate the earth. It is apparently not enough to honor our religious forefathers who struggled with spiritual matters and see the symbolism in many biblical stories. The biblical inerrant dogmatists require that we abandon science, reason, and common sense to be right with God or face their wrath. As previously mentioned, creation scientists are the only so-called scientists who try to pass laws that require their special theory to be taught in public schools. It is the only "scientific" theory embraced and promoted by fundamentalists. It could be abandoned if they awaken to the fact that it does not take the Bible literally. In the meantime they both declare war on academic science and the secular.

Besides creation science, there is Christian Science and Scientology to suggest science is into spiritual matters. Mary Baker Eddy (1821–1910) wrote *Science and Health with Key to the Scriptures* and the message emphasized healing by prayer. As a boy I read where even compound fractures healed through Christian Science, but distant neighbors of ours died in prayer over conditions physicians could treat. The father of a friend of mine who was killed in WWII joined the religion because he was told that his son still resided in their home. Since WWII I have met several good people who were Christian Scientists that nevertheless went to physicians for medical problems, like the movie actress Doris Day has done. Mark Twain wrote a scathing report on the religion titled *Christian Science* (pub. 1907) that didn't seem to have much effect. I believe, however, that it is the first religion to connect the word *science* to spiritual matters. Scientology is the most recent. The Church of Scientology was founded in 1954 by L. Ron Hubbard who wrote science fiction but realized that we are all spirits going back some 75 million years and that with proper counseling we can get the spirit right (CA 1/30/00). The counseling is done by 14,000 volunteer ministers who study the Scientology Handbook and as one declared, they "can do something about any situation in life" (CA 2/9/02). Their headquarters is at Clearwater where they first called themselves United Churches of Florida, and they have lots of money. In 1975 the FBI showed that Scientology planned to control city government. City officials then passed laws in 1982 requiring churches to disclose their finances, but Scientologist lawyers got the laws overturned. For twenty-six years the IRS refused them tax-exempt status but in 1993 gave up the expensive fight waged by lawyers (CA 3/9/00). At present they are spending over one million dollars on billboard advertising indicating that no matter what problem we have they have an answer (CA 2/9/02). Scientologists oppose psychology and psychiatry because Hubbard knew that religious philosophy offered a better way to happiness. The daughter of Elvis Presley, Lisa Marie, indicated to television viewers that the philosophy is designed to achieve physical and mental well-being. Indeed, movie stars like John Travolta and Tom Cruise are strong adherents (CA 1/30/00). But Bob Minton of Clearwater declares it a cult and culpable in the death of a former member (CA 1/30/00). The French government declares Scientology to be a sect that makes money by swindle and is trying to put the sect out of business. One Frenchwoman, for example, was pressured to take out a $6,000 loan which drove her husband to suicide, and in Marseilles five Scientologists were found guilty of swindle (CA 3/4/00). The French also don't like the Order of the Solar Temple that lost seventy-four members to suicide. The German government considers the Scientology group subversive (shades of Clearwater?) and is also trying to put these religious philosophers out of business. But Tom Cruise, a former amateur wrestler and well-known movie star, is trying to change the spirit of the Germans. He recently asked the U.S. ambassador to Germany to join the fight on behalf of Scientology (CA 2/4/02). It seems to be a religion of money, litigation, and man-made spirituality.

I have heard Billy Graham say that Christ may return to earth at any time, and Jerry Falwell some years ago said that he would not be surprised if Jesus returned in the year 2000 when many others were certain He would. Many evangelicals hold that He will return only after everyone becomes a Christian while other evangelicals are certain that this will occur only after the Jews control Jerusalem and rebuild the old Temple of Solomon. Then Christians will be saved before Armageddon, as espoused by Ed McAteer and his ilk (David Waters, CA 8/21/02). McAteer started the Moral Majority movement and is now making news again as leader of the Evangelical Friend of Israel movement. He and his kind would make government an instrument of religion and would dictate foreign policy for their fanciful religious notion. While the likes of Washington, Polk, the Roosevelts, and Harry Truman would most likely ignore their views, it is said that political leaders of 2002 are very attentive (CA 8/21/02). I believe many would feel more comfortable if they would listen to leaders of the Salvation Army or other less vociferous, militant groups. The simple idea that Christ won't return until someone builds a temple apparently appeals to millions of voters but not to the silent Christian majority. Even McAteer does not know whether "Jesus is coming tomorrow or 5,000 years from now," but he is certain about his mission to fulfill his agenda to rebuild Solomon's Temple. At age seventy-six the cost of his mission does not seem to concern him.

There is no reason to believe and certainly no proof that Jesus would applaud people killing each other so that He could see a temple. The dogma is foreign to most Christian faiths, but these do not take to the airways and support politics like the Christian Right. McAteer is a retired salesman who says he is not modest but is honest. He and his ilk sound more like arrogant and adamant. No science can explain how religious salesmen can fashion a fanciful spiritual story into a notable political action movement with the support of millions. Hopefully the whispers of the silent Christian majority will eventually draw more political attention than the vociferous ones so that common sense may prevail. But now in 2002 the president wants to use tax income to fund the good work of religious groups and 100 congressmen wish to pass laws that enable churches to enter politics without losing their tax-exempt status, as reported by David Walters (CA 8/21/02). The idea is to give money to a church as a tax deduction to help a favorite politician while obtaining federal tax dollars for the church to help the needy. Pastor D. James Kennedy thinks that thousands of ministers are afraid their churches would face the IRS if they spoke politically for a favorite candidate. If so, the IRS is helping the ministers to focus on what the New Testament teaches us about government and religion.

The case of David Koresh and the Davidians also demonstrate the fanciful nature of religion. His followers knew that Koresh was "God made flesh" and spoke through him (CA 6/29/00). He was hostile to government that agrees with the symbolic depiction of a demonic, dictatorial government in Revelations 13, but contrasts with the teachings of Jesus (John 19:11), Paul (Romans 13:1–5), and Peter (1 Peter 2:17). The Davidians started in 1935 when they were excommunicated from the Seventh-Day Adventist that was founded in the 1840s (*Handbook of Denominations the United States*, 10th ed., 1995). The founder William Miller predicted unsuccessfully that Christ would return October 22, 1844. He must have thought he was God, for Christ clearly stated that no one but God would know when he would return, not even angels (Matthew 24:36). Miller first predicted

Christ's return in the spring of 1844, but studied the Bible and found an error in his calculations. It is written that at least 50,000 people prayerfully waited to see Jesus on October 22, and afterward most returned to their former churches. Another Miller (Monte Kim Miller) of Colorado predicted in 1998 doomsday to be February 15, 2002, on the 777th of God's 7th millennium (CA 2/19/02). Earlier Miller predicted he would die on the streets of Jerusalem in December 1999 and rise from the dead three days later (Perre Magness, CA 12/30/99). In Africa a former Roman Catholic, Kibweteere, predicted the world's end on December 31, 1999, after which he predicted it to end a year later. In between, he and 250 members of Restore the Ten Commandments feasted and then went up in flames (CA 3/19/00). Koresh and his Davidians established a theocracy in Texas and acquired many weapons. They had planned to be among the 144,000 people that an angel would place a mark on their foreheads to be God's servants (Revelations 7:3–8) prior to Armageddon (Revelations 16:16). They also, sadly, arranged to go up in flames rather than submit to the laws of man (CA 7/11/00). Scholars disagree about the location of Armageddon, but a male angel will dry up the Euphrates River so the forces of good can march unimpeded (Revelations 16:12). Charles Taze Russell in 1884 organized what is now called Jehovah's Witnesses on the knowledge that Christ would soon come and that 144,000 pure people would be selected to rule with God after Armageddon. The 144,000, however, will be from the twelve tribes of Israel and will be a choir in heaven (Revelations 7:4-8; 14:3). On television Jack Van Impe has joyfully told us about the end of the world for many years, as have others. In recent years books on the coming of Christ were best-sellers and a movie, *Left Behind*, on the subject entertained millions. The subject seemed to have replaced visitation by aliens. Perhaps with the passing of the millennium the frenzy will end, although in 2001 an advertisement titled "Christ Is Coming Very Soon!" was declared History's Greatest Event (CA 4/5/01).

But LaHaye and other fundamentalists have been getting out the Good News to us before it is too late. David Waters suggested that since the end is near there was no point in profiting from the movie or the 25 million doomsday books sold (CA 2/18/01). One cynic said, "Forget Armageddon, we go to work Monday." Alas, some don't wait for the end. Marshall Herff Applewhite and thirty-nine Heaven's Gate followers killed themselves in 1997 after packing suitcases to catch a ride on a rocket hidden behind the comet Hale-Bopp (CA 4/28/97).

Jim Jones in 1978, with 913 followers, hastened their ascent to heaven with cyanide and gunshot after killing the inquisitive Congressman Leo Ryan in Jonestown, Guyana (CA 4/1/00). The Outer Dimensional Forces, members founded by Orville Gordon of Texas, have declared that heavenly allies would soon flood the USA and whisk them away to safety (CA 12/30/99). After Martin Luther (1483–1546) started the Reformation, hundreds of denominations sprang up (*Handbook of Denominations in the United States*, 1995). Each appeals to someone's fancy. The Jehovah's Witnesses were among the first (1884) to perceive Satan's work in false churches, human government, and oppressive business and so refuse to participate in politics, salute our flag, or bear arms in war. Others like the Christadelphians hold similar views. They all expect Armageddon soon.

Religious services also provide evidence that religion is fanciful. Most services are dignified, somber, and/or happy, but on television stations like TBN the style and messages used by preachers vary from dignified to performing jazz for Jesus. At the end of the program they request love offerings and/or sell earth-shaking books and videos, for religion to many is big money. *The London Times* (March 29, p. 32) reported that in 1984 Jerry Falwell received some 45 million dollars in donations and that Oral Roberts did as well (perhaps a million people gave on average 45 dollars?). Some preachers conduct uplifting interviews while others appear as corrupt as the old defunct Jim and Tammy Baker show. They divorced and he went to jail for fraud after collecting millions. They even displayed on TV their magnificent home and their air-conditioned doghouse. Some preachers stomp their feet, shout and sweat while others instantly heal medical problems by prayer. Most place their hand on the ill person's head to heal, but one guy thumps the forehead, after which the patient falls backward. The patient is caught by others, presumably to avoid injury. One jolly preacher boasted that he cured a walleyed blind boy that caused the boy's mother to faint. He also said he cured a child of spina bifida and saw the scars behind the child's head vanish! The audience loved it. Oral Roberts vividly recalls causing a crushed foot to become normal as his first medical miracle. He recently had heart surgery, but for many years healed others. As early as 1955 he took in 3 million dollars selling books, lapel pins, and other items. Several years later a diabetic woman died three days after discarding insulin, believing she had been cured by Roberts (*The People's Almanac*, 1975). By 1966 he stopped faith healing on TV but built a prayer tower, a university, and a medical school in Tulsa. The medical school failed. A former dean at my medical school, from 1975 to 1977, Charles B. McCall, was said to have been selected to head the Tulsa school of medicine because he did not drink, smoke or swear, and was lean. Around 1948 Roberts would ask his radio listeners to lay hands on their receivers to obtain a point of contact with the Lord. Today Pat Robertson heals the ailments of some by telepathic prayer. Those he helped send him a card or letter of gratitude. A reader of Marilyn Vos Savant asked her why the TV religious healers don't relieve the suffering seen in hospitals. Indeed, all infections, all strokes, all cancers, spinal injuries, and other afflictions could be cured without much expense. Her answer was to be amused as they have no such power and become ill themselves (*Parade*, CA 6/19/02). Richard Feynman made the point that those who believe in faith healing won't need science and that if miracles do cure, the phenomenon should be studied scientifically to improve upon the incidence of success (*The Pleasure of Finding Things Out*, 1999). One experiment might be to take all emergency cases of compound fractures, gunshot wounds, third-degree burns, and the like to faith healers to ascertain their healing ability.

Sometimes unsolicited miracles occur, as in the case of divine dentistry in Texas. While attending a church revival dozens of people noted that their less expensive dental work of crowns, plates, bridges, and fillings had turned to gold. It was reported that since the 1980s this phenomenon took place in other countries. One dentist, however, wondered why God didn't correct the problem rather than cover the defect with gold (CA 1/6/00). The most bizarre, successful worship service was evidently conducted by Billy Sunday (1862–1935). Sunday had been a professional baseball player who turned to preaching. During the service he would shadowbox with the Devil or imitate a sinner trying to steal first base with God calling him out. He would tell the audience how David socked Goliath between the lamps to go down for the count. While sermonizing he would skip, fall down, and imitate drunkards, society women and moral backsliders. Clergymen criticized him for turning worship into vaudeville but recognized that he got results. For several summers I worked with Elmer Rose who once heard Sunday preach in the steel city of Gary, Indiana. Elmer said Sunday asked all the women present to cross their legs. He then said, "Now the gates to Hell are closed." The audience roared. In 1917 he became a millionaire from the offerings of 98,264 people of New York City who had been converted to Christ (*The People's Almanac*, 1975). Sunday left Memphis in the spring of 1924 with a personal fund of $20,130 after condemning modernism, evolution, pacifism, Bolshevism, ecclesiastical crooks, jazz, and junk before some 86,000 listeners (Robert A. Lanier, *Memphis in the Twenties*, 1979). Aimee Semple McPhearson (1890–1944) raised even more millions when workers were well off, earning five dollars per day. She accidentally became a faith healer when while preaching an old lady left her wheelchair and others did likewise. In 1923 she spent $1,500,000 to build a temple of worship that also displayed crutches, braces, and wheelchairs that the faithful left behind after their cure. She humbly explained that she was only a little office girl that Jesus used to heal others (*The People's Almanac*, 1975). She did not explain how Jesus used her to obtain a divorce and fool around with a married man. Although her popularity waned with scandal, she still entertained many in her temple of worship until she committed suicide at age fifty-four. McPhearson is one among many preachers who show that there is big money in religion. One televangelist said that denominationalism may be about market share.

In the year 2000, 74.3 billion dollars was given to 353,000 houses of worship (*Giving USA 2001*, 46th Annual Issue). This does not include funds spent on social services, religious books and money sent to the televangelists. In 1989 there were 1,052 radio stations devoting at least twenty hours per week to religion (*American and the Mass Media* ed. Q.J. Schultz, 1990). Someone said that that was to fill the holes in our heads. Alec Foege describes in his book *The Empire Gold Built* (Pub. 1996) that Pat Robertson takes in annually $295 million for one foundation, $36 million for another, and $12 million for a third. He also has 1,400 students enrolled in his university, owns a TV station (CBN), and reportedly has one million TV viewers. If all those viewers are members of the 700 Club, Robertson would receive $240 million per year for it costs only $20 per month (less than one dollar per day) to be a member. Robertson also accepts tithing. Recently (May 2002) I saw several witness say that tithing to his ministry brought financial rewards. Perhaps local churches lack that kind of power. It looks like his ministries could take in at least 600 million dollars yearly. And there are hundreds of electric churches. Viewers in western Michigan gave on average $339 a year to TV evangelists (*Televangelists and American Culture* by Q.J. Shultz, 1991). Billy Graham is among several hundred electronic churches that issue financial reports of their expenditures; but since this is not required by law, most televangelists report their expenditures "to nobody but God," as described by Larry Martz in the book *Ministry of Greed*, 1988. Martz tells us that Jim and Tammy Bakker reported only to

God and were taking in $129 million per year, and once raised $30 million in one week, until it was clear that they were crooks and Jim was caught in an affair with Jessica Hahn, the Bible Belle. Jerry Falwell thought that what Jim did was the greatest cancer in the 2000-year history of Christianity, but Falwell hardly qualifies as an historian and also did not disclose his expenditures to the public. One ploy of the electronic church is to make an appeal for a specific amount of money, like $200,000 to feed the hungry, and any extra that is received is gravy. Rozelle Frankl points out that programs of the tax-exempt electric (electronic) churches cover such topics as marriage, medicine, news, public policy and politics (*Televangelism—The Marketing of Popular Religion*, 1987). Electric ministers judge for us as to who are true believers. Frankl states that our Founding Fathers envisioned religion as personal and spiritual, not social and political. Although the total dollars spent on religion seems to be unknown, every style of worship finds an audience. While the rules of algebra are finite and universal, religious services are as we like it.

God may have lied to Moses on purpose or to show us that he can change his mind. God told Moses that, "man may not see me and live" (Exodus 33:20). Yet Jacob wrestled with God and was worried because he said at Peniel, "I have seen God face to face and yet my life is spared" (Genesis 32:30). The parents of Samson, Manoah and wife, entertained an angel of the Lord who Manoah later recognized as God. Manoah was also worried for he said, "We shall surely die, because we have seen God" (Judges 13:22). Another witness, Micaiah, makes it clear that he saw God sitting on his throne in heaven, but was not worried (1 Kings 22:19), and Isaiah saw God on his throne wearing a robe and being attended by seraphim (Isaiah 6:1-2). I do not believe that any of the biblical authors meant to intentionally contradict Moses, but such contradictions indicate that the Bible was not written to be flawless history or logic. The inerrant biblical scholar declares otherwise.

Christianity sustains me but the New Testament is not based on logic or science. The story that Jesus was conceived by God as his only begotten son and that he was truly a human who died by design for our sins separates Christianity from all other religions. As a human, Jesus often sends mixed messages, if taken literally. Jesus tells us that he is God's only begotten son (John 3:16), but Luke (3:38) lists Adam as the Son of God. They differ, however, in that Adam came from dust while Jesus came from DNA and proteins to give us the means for everlasting life (John 3:16). He tells his first converts to only preach to the people of Israel, not gentiles or Samaritans (Matthew 10:5); but later, after he died, tells them to make disciples in all nations (Matthew 28:19). He reminds us to obey the commandment to honor our parents (Mark 7:10) but tells us we must hate our parents and other loved ones to be his disciple (Luke 14:26). Jesus tells us to pluck out our eye if what we see has caused sin (Mark 9:47, Matthew 5:29 and 18:9) and lose a hand if it caused sin (Mark 9:43). To my knowledge, no fundamentalist takes these edicts literally. He tells us to pray to God in secret in a closet and avoid repetitious prayers as heathens do (Matthew 6:6-7, KJV). Taken literally, this means prayer is forbidden in church, in the desert, on the battlefield, or anywhere unless we take along a closet. Billy Graham (CA 12/18/77) argues that its all right to pray in public because Jesus did (John 6:11), but that ignores what he said. Jesus tells us to forgive our brothers who sin 7x70 times (Matthew 18:22), yet to excommunicate transgressors from the church as heathens (Matthew 18:17 KJV, TLB). This admonition to remove sinners from church is repeated by Paul (1 Corinthians 5:2). Taken together, it looks as though a church member must literally sin 490 times before excommunication. He tells us to love our neighbor but that he did not come for peace but to cause strife and division among family members (Luke 12:51-53). He also said that he was not good (Mark 10:18), yet wants us to be his disciples. He declares the old Mosaic law of revenge—an eye for an eye, etc.—is wrong. Rather we must let someone strike both cheeks, not just one, and not contest lawsuits (Matthew 5:38–40). We are also to bless and pray for those who curse us and persecute us and to love our enemies (Matthew 5:44).

If we use the aforementioned argument of Billy Graham to follow his example, it becomes evident that Jesus did not suffer evildoers, persecutors, and repeat sinners. Jesus the Christ saved an adulteress from being stoned and told her to "go and sin no more" (John 8:11). He cured a man of illness and told him to "sin no more, that nothing worse befall you" (John 5:14, RSV). In Jerusalem he displayed no love for the merchants who had turned God's Temple into a den of thieves. He physically drove them out of the Temple and knocked over their stalls (Luke 19:45-46; Matthew 21:12-13). He called the Pharisees hypocrites, serpents, and blind fools (Matthew 23:13-33). He rejects totally false prophets and evildoers, stating, "depart from me, ye that work iniquity" (Matthew 7:23, KJV). In more modem terms he is quoted as saying, "Go away, for your deeds are evil" (TLB). Moreover, Jesus told his disciples not to waste their blessings on ungodly people (Matthew 10:13, TLB) and explains the three simple steps to excommunicate church members (Matthew 18:15–17 TLB). In Revelation (the last book of the Bible where an angel tells John what to expect real soon, 1:1-3, and which today some pretend to understand) Jesus said that he hated the Nicolaitans (Revelation 2:6), which was a group of Christian heretics, and said that he would kill any children of Jezebel because of her evil fornication (Revelations 2:20-23). If so, he could hate and kill the innocent. In a more reasonable vein, he explained that sinners must repent to be forgiven (Luke 13:5). Therefore, contrary to popular belief, the victim of assault need not forgive unless the offender repents. Indeed, forgiveness is basic to Christianity; but if someone causes injury, we need not automatically forgive repeated attacks, 490 times. Christ was no softie. From the Old Testament, he gave us only six commandments for harmonious relationships (Matthew 19:18, KJV). Although he taught that many of the tedious religious rules of the Old Testament were unnecessary to enter heaven, he never rejected nor extolled execution as punishment (Numbers 35:30; Deuteronomy 24:16).

We can only fancy what he looked like without photographs. Mark (6:3) said he was a carpenter. Some fancy him to be muscular, as depicted by Titian in his painting of 1559, *The Entombment*, for in those days carpenters did masonry. It seems unlikely that he was as emaciated as most artists portray him, as skin and bones. He left us nothing in his writing, but scholars say he spoke the language of commoners, Aramaic, and that an early book of his sayings was lost. Nevertheless, many undated, unnamed Gospels were used by early church members that dealt with the life of Christ. Then around A.D. 150 church leaders selected four and gave them names, like Matthew, and declared them Scripture (*Adult Bible Studies*, Teacher, Vol. 8: No. 2, 1999-2000). One biblical fundamentalist, Brian H. Edwards, also states that none of the original writings exist today and that many copies were made from copies. Then he states that, "there is a good reason why God allowed all of the original manuscripts to be destroyed." The reason was that God must have found errors (*Nothing but the Truth*, Evangelical Press, 1993). Edwards declares, therefore, that God acted like an English professor who corrected the manuscripts of students until perfection was achieved. I have heard fundamentalists distort stories like that of Jonah and the fish (Jonah 1:17) and of God wrestling Jacob all night (Genesis 32:24-30) to fit their fancy.

To alter biblical stories to make them more palatable is deception. To declare that all Biblical statements are historically and scientifically correct, without error, is a lie. There is no sin in doubting, only lying. One of the great Biblical lessons is about doubting Thomas (John 20:25-27). Jesus did not forsake him for doubting the resurrection—he seemed to expect it. Jesus never said thou shall not doubt, but gave us two to eleven rules for living that if everyone adhered to we could leave our homes unlocked and give anyone a ride in our automobiles. Trust and freedom are products of his rules. Being able to trust family members and neighbors frees us from much worry. If no one stole, we need not worry about shoplifters or stockbrokers. We could trust anyone with our money and daughters. He left us with beautiful parables that have great meaning for better living, more so than the Aesop fables. "In God We Trust" means nothing unless we are trustworthy. The message of Jesus, it seems, is to make neighbors and communities better and to comfort us with hope. He did not, evidently, consider males with crushed testis (Deuteronomy 23:1-2) or those who touched a dead pig (Deuteronomy 14:8) to be unworthy. The laws he took from the Old Testament all foster civility. He even worked on the Sabbath that was supposed to be deadly (Exodus 31:15). More timely, he explained that our souls are not harmed by what we eat, but by what we think and say (Mark 7:15). Billy Graham momentarily forgot this lesson when he wanted to do something with President Nixon to destroy the strangle-hold Jews had on our news media (CA 3/7/02). Graham apparently thought his soul was tarnished by the remark made thirty years earlier for which he publicly apologized (CA 3/3/02).

Political power and wealth has corrupted religion and religion has corrupted reason. The latter was evident in a recent engrossing documentary of a modem witch-hunt in Gilmore, Texas, seen on the program *Dateline* (CA 3/8/02). The state appointed four Christians, who seemed qualified, to investigate the disappearance of a woman and a possible cover-up by a local police officer. By coercion and torment the investigators recorded on tape their evidence of satanic rituals where babies were eaten and the missing woman was killed. A truck driver and the officer took part, among others, as proven by witnesses, including a seven-year-old boy. The father of the missing girl was absolutely certain that the policeman was innocent, but the witch-hunt continued. Eventually some sane people in law enforcement got involved and found that the truck driver had to be in New York at the time of the witchcraft ceremony, that more babies were eaten than could be produced by anyone at the time, and that there was no physical signs of any Satanic ritual, in agreement with what the accused officer first reported. All of the accused had been jailed but were freed by the sane. The tape recordings first recorded the voices of sane people—including the seven year old—but later became bizarre. When asked about the lack of forensic evidence in the case, the reply from the first investigating team was that the absence of evidence was proof of witchcraft. These Christian social morons applied superstition to solve a forensic problem.

Thousands make the same denial about science. If anything is shown to be more than ten thousand years old, it must be witchcraft. A belief system can deny reality because it is based on belief. How beliefs become facts to the believer is a mystery. It was reported that some would pay $200 for a bowl of tiger penis soup and that one pound of powdered rhino horn sells for $25,000 (CA 3/25/01). At one time syphilis and plague was attributed to God's wrath (CA 4/13/99) and several years ago Jerry Falwell thought the same of AIDS. He later apologized. But today many clergymen wish to make the point that the remarkable advances in surgery and medicine are by God's blessing. Periodically I even hear some preachers telling their audience how to prevent and cure cancer with prayer. I have not heard specific prayer instruction for the prevention of or cure for heart attack, diverticulitis, pyorrhea, cleft palate, gallstones, parkinsonism, acromegaly, diabetes, hemophilia, malaria, amyotrophic lateral sclerosis, and countless other afflictions—perhaps because their audience is more frightened of cancer. Those who praise God for modern medicine ignore the fact that many scientific and medical marvels of today were discovered by men who were not Christians—even atheists—so that God must favor the intellect over religion.

Jesus is quoted as saying, "Whatever you ask in my name, I shall grant it and if you ask anything in my name, I shall grant it" (John 14:13-14, RSV). If this is nothing but the truth, it seems that Stephen died unnecessarily from the stoning sought by Saul—later called Paul (Acts 7:55-58). Perhaps Stephen had not heard of this declaration or maybe he wished to be the first to die in the name of Christ. In any case, if it is nothing but the truth, life would be effortless if anything we prayed for in his name was granted. The problems of farmers, teachers, policemen, and others would immediately dissolve upon request. With this prayer everyone could be wealthy, though Christ states that we will "always have the poor with you" (Matthew 26:11). He did not specifically exclude miscreants from praying to him, so the wishes of criminals might also be fulfilled. If so, the prayers of the bad guys and good people could collide. The message of Christ, taught by most clergy and in Sunday schools, to be compassionate toward children, adults in trouble, and the poor is beautiful. He shows us ever-lasting life and we think of him perfect in spirit. Those that wrote of him long after his death, however, were apparently not perfect scribes nor concerned with the logic proposed by Aristotle. Who during our Great Depression of the 1930s, or any economic depression, would have remained poor if the promise attributed to Jesus, by scribes, to fulfill any need was accurate?

Some investigators have recently tried to understand how the brain produces spirituality. For many years neurosurgeons have known that electrical stimulation of different areas of the brain will elicit visual, tactile, auditory, and other hallucinations where the conscious patient may even see and hear a friend or relative speak and sing. Recently an area of the brain was located (angular gyrus of the parietal lobe) where stimulation always produced an out-of-body experience (CA 9/19/01). The patient saw herself while looking down from the ceiling. A Canadian group placed magnetized helmets on five adults and four reported they experienced someone like God or evil standing nearby. Others studied brain scans of Tibetan Buddhists during meditation and found that the frontal cortex (important for concentration and conscientiousness) to be very active while areas of the parietal lobe (concerned with self-awareness) were markedly reduced in activity (CA 6/24/01). Other groups studied the effect the psychedelic psilocybin (Mexican magic mushroom) had during a religious service and also studied the effect of temporal lobe seizures (psychomotor epilepsy) or hypnosis on spirituality (*Science News* 159:104-106, 2001). The psilo-cybin definitely enhanced the spirituality of the religious service: they saw colors and felt a oneness with God. Some with epilepsy or under hypnosis reported having a spiritual experience.

Some theologians felt such experiments were demeaning because the results suggested God was a product of the brain. It could also be argued that God put a mechanism in the head so that we could get in tune with Him, but where else would religion be located but in the head? Some have posited that great religious visionaries may have suffered from epilepsy, but in any case it seems that spiritual experi-ences are rather common, especially to those trained in religion. John Wesley (1703–1791), for instance, had been a preacher for years (even in America) but felt the presence of God because of a warm feeling in his heart at Aldersgate, London. A wonderful elderly lady once calmly told two of us that while walking along a lake her recent-ly deceased husband joined her and they briefly conversed—he essentially said all was okay. She never repeated the story, pays her taxes, and by any criteria is not a religious zealot. I have had vivid dreams (in black and white) of conversing with deceased loved ones, but none in my family have talked to the dead while awake.

Nevertheless, 84 percent of Americans believe in divine miracles and 48 percent say they experienced a miracle (CA 4/23/00). Miracles seem to be events we cannot explain, like surviving a battle or a devastating car crash when 50,000 others perished. Others call it luck. Many scientists attribute their success to luck, like having a good teacher or using a newly invented instrument to make a pivotal discovery (*The Neurosciences: Paths of Discovery*, 1975). Louis Pasteur (1822–1895), however, said that luck favors the prepared mind, but he was speaking about science. When a tornado just misses one's home, that is another kind of luck, or a miracle. Rather than luck, the religious are more likely to call a desirable outcome or pleasant event a blessing, and poor results bad luck.

Neuroscientists have identified systems in the brain important to cognitive functions relating to reality and fancy. These involve structures like the cerebral cortex, the amygdala, nucleus accumbens, and the midbrain ventral tegmentum which involve at least the neurotransmitters gamma aminobutyric acid, acetylcholine, glutamic acid, serotonin, and dopamine. By activation (volition) of one system or the other, we may daydream or do the income tax. The effect of dopamine on the nucleus accumbens is to favor fancy and an excess of dopamine causes psychosis, at least one cause. The child, however, cannot separate a dream or a daydream from reality as easily as experienced adults. A spooky movie can be real to a child while enjoyable to an adult. When movies were new, the appearance of a train coming at the audience, ever expanding, caused some to leave their seats in terror. Probably everyone uses the fancy system to relax, perhaps to excess by some, for it seems to be the easiest system to activate. I have known successful scientist who periodically become engrossed in music, movies, western novels, and sports. Indeed, it is evident that some spectators lose themselves completely to wild abandonment during sporting events when their favorite just barely wins. They lose their self-image for a moment. And logic plays no role in romantic passion or rage. Great thinkers must inherit a great reality system, like we inherit right-handedness, for they take to learning like ducks take to water. For most the fancy system takes little effort, common in teenagers, and will not let facts disturb opinions. Many make up their minds and lose their heads. This wishful system makes us vulnerable for what appeals to us seems to be true.

The great question is how stories of supernatural phenomena become real in the minds of millions, not how electromagnetic forces can produce an eerie experience. Part of the answer is by rote, like tying shoes or doing addition. Most will adhere to the religion of their parents and community, be it Catholic, Hindu, Islam, Judaism, Voodoo, or whatever. Even in this modern day 75 percent of the Amish children keep their faith as adults (CA 3/21/01). The Amish, Orthodox Jew, Jehovah's Witnesses, and Mormons, however, will ignore those who leave the faith as though they did not exist. This insanity is called shunning (CA 12/28/01). Our great early leaders, like Washington and Lincoln, should have taught us by now that all good persons are welcome, not shunned, be they Irish Catholic or Jew (CA 8/19/00). Electromagnetism or epilepsy fail to explain how John Philip Walker, who was reared a Catholic, became Sulayman al-Faris the Taliban fighter (CA 12/3/01) or why some join the International Society for Krishna Consciousness (CA 2/20/01). Science cannot explain why throwing the ashes of former Beatle George Harrison into the holy water of the Ganges River will release his soul heavenward (CA 12/4/01) or why Buddhist monks prayed for seven days to save the souls 1.3 million killed diseased chickens (CA 1/1/98) and why Hindu rituals were performed for thirty monkeys killed accidentally on high-voltage wires (CA 8/17/96). Someone said that the brain is the engine of reason and the seat of the soul. It may be a long while before anyone can explain how the soul replaces reason.

One place the intellect may influence the souls is in adult Bible classes that are commonly sponsored by many churches. Patriotic war veterans and citizens of all persuasion meet in civility to consider different aspects of the Bible with the help of printed lessons as a guide. A volunteer teacher deals with the lessen and in so-called moderate churches may consider as unimportant whether Jonah in fact lived inside a fish underwater for three days compared to the moral the study is supposed to convey. The fundamentalists call this "modernism." Indeed, the biblical inerrant dogmatist Brian H. Edwards argues that all stories in Genesis (he particularly mentions Jonah) are historically correct and to think otherwise says we have "abandoned sound principles of interpretation." He worries that if we use common sense to reject part of the Noah story, we must reject the well-documented story of the resurrection of Christ. The fundamentalist, however, must abandon common sense and reason to declare as historically correct that the sun moved backward and that an ass spoke to Balaam. It seems obvious that our Bible is a history of people struggling with the problems of life and longing for divine guidance. We can honor their struggle and even empathize, without abandoning reason.

Modernism is not a modern phenomenon. Our second president, John Adams (1797–1801) slavishly attended the Congregational Church but reportedly had contempt for Christian orthodoxy (CA 7/21/01). One book lists Adams as a Unitarian along with Isaac Newton and other thinkers. One definition of a Unitarian is a Ph.D. who goes to church. Perhaps the ultimate modernist was our third president, Thomas Jefferson (1801-1809). Jefferson extirpated all references to miracles and mystery in the life of Jesus and pieced together the parables and aphorisms. He wrote John Adams that it was like removing diamonds from a dunghill and that the edited story of Jesus was "the most sublime and benevolent code of morals which has ever been offered to man" (Richard N. Ostling, CA 7/21/01). Christians will agree with that conclusion but not necessarily with its derivation. Jefferson never published his personal Bible for he felt religion was a personal matter. That feeling seemed common in those days. George Washington and others wanted to deal with the trustworthy, for a man was as good as his word, not his religion. The Jefferson Bible, however, was published in 1906 by our Government Printing Office and presented to new congressmen.

In contrast to Jefferson, many need mystery in religion, just as spirituality is mysterious. Indeed, Billy Graham declares that "angels are real" (CA 11/24/00) and millions agree and purchase books on the subject. One survey indicated that a third of born-again baby boomer Christians believe in reincarnation and astrology (CA 1/22/00). The crown prince of Thailand, Maha Varjiralongkorn, used astrologers recently to plan his wedding (CA 2/4/01) and our former first lady, now Senator Hilary R. Clinton, used a sacred psychologist, Jean Houston, to chat with Eleanor Roosevelt in 1996 (CA 1/22/00). Astrology must be big business for it is available in books, daily in newspapers, and on the Internet, though God condemns star worshippers to death (Deuteronomy 17:2-5). Certainly religion is also big business, with tax-free benefits. Recently (3/9/02) I heard and saw Robert Schuler on the Hour of Power selling for $240 bird statues to help his ministry. Televangelists sell all kinds of items and if a million viewers sent only one dollar that would be a good day's work. The trick is convincing viewers that the preacher is doing society and us a favor. Some like Carl Baugh (Ph.D.) work for God by demonizing science while others demonize all secular schools for corrupting our youth (forget the movies). A clinical psychologist I knew said that one remarkable characteristic of personal faith is that it will go any-where—to war or college. The secular teacher will not harm our youth with facts and don't have to teach them that angels are real to be good citizens.

Government is a new source of tax-exempt revenue for recognized religious groups. For twenty years the International Society for Krishna Consciousness has received millions from our government to help the unfortunate and feed them vegetarian diets (Laurie Goodstein, CA 2/20/01). This group, also known as the Hare Krishna religion (remember the monks at the airport?) may go bankrupt this year because of lawsuits for sexual and physical abuse in their boarding schools, which are now closed (CA 2/9/02). In February of 2001 the USA Office of Faith Based and Community Initiative opened to further help religious groups to help those in need. Some feel that the Salvation Army and Catholic Charities would use the money responsibly, but worry that the Hare Krishna, Church of Scientology, Reverend Sun Myung Moon, and others might use the money to strengthen themselves more than the unfortunate (CA 2/20/01). One Jewish group alleges that federal dollars are being spent on religious instruction in some public schools and are suing to halt the practice (CA 10/4/02).

The wall separating church and state that Thomas Jefferson spoke of to Connecticut Baptists in 1802 is apparently crumbling. Since the 1960s politicking, name calling, and greed in the name of God has increasingly gained popular support. Recently many preachers exhorted their followers to give part or all of a recent tax rebate of $300 to $600 to their religion and one said, "It's not our money, it's God's" (CA 7/30/01). Since the total rebate for 2001 was 38 billion dollars, the asking was bigger than it seemed. The guy selling refrigerators to live might want some of the money also. Most clergy who serve our communities, I believe, earn our support for the services and comfort they provide church members. But Jesus would most likely look askance at the opulence and arrogance displayed by many televangelists. All his life Jesus was poor. He was born in a stable and was buried in a borrowed grave. He sent his close disciples out to spread his message and told them not to take money nor even extra clothes (Matthew 10:9-10). They were not on a mission to impress the wealthy and powerful. Jesus also said that we cannot love God and money at the same time (Matthew 6:24). Paul left us a similar admonition (Hebrews 13:8). The idea is that when we love money there is never enough, so said Solomon (Ecclesiastes 4:10).

Jesus said, however, that the disciples could expect to have their needs fulfilled by the people they serve, so someone had to have some wealth. Paul, however, took his own course. He worked for money to pay for the necessities of life, admonished us to avoid lazy Christians, and said that those who do not work shall not eat (2 Thessalonians 3:9–10).

The study of the Bible or Bibles brings us in touch with the past, shared by George Washington, our ancestors, parents, and friends. It can give us a perspective of life that is less self-centered. It can, and usually does, promote civility and trustworthiness. Collectively the church can be a community of caring—I know it serves that function for many. The church can promote feelings of belonging, dignity, and security—especially valuable to children. Churches can, and do, serve as fixed centers of celebration, comfort, and hope. They are also avenues of cheerfulness and joy for many. Indeed, Christ admonished his followers to be of good cheer. For many, religion is a source of kind words and good works. Churches serve our spiritual needs, for man seems to be the only animal that harbors the wish for eternal life and uses some rules to insure its fulfillment. But finally spirituality is a personal matter that by all reports is achieved in countless ways. History and newspaper articles also show that many identified as religious are liars, greedy, cruel, and insane. These human traits are not confined to religion but history is replete with stories of the selfish leading the willing in the name of God. The theologian Bruce Vawter argued that declaring the Bible inerrant in all matters shows contempt for God's gift of intellect. That is one opinion of God, but with certainty, to claim that our Bible is perfect in history and perfect in science is to abandon reason. To discard reason is to dishonor God.

CHAPTER 13

Blissful Ignorance

I ONCE MENTIONED TO AN ELDERLY FRIEND OF OUR FAMILY THAT THE TWO creation stories in Genesis explain why Cain so easily found a wife in Nod. She adamantly said that her Bible did not have two creation stories when in fact it did. Men and women were created on the sixth day in God's image, but for most only the story told later about Adam is fixed in their minds and glorified in paint and sculpture by Michelangelo Buonarroti (1475-1564). This friend has been a devout Catholic all her life but shares with countless other Christians a blissful ignorance of Scripture. I once mentioned to a Jewish colleague that God gave the name Israel to Jacob only after they had wrestled all night (Genesis 32:30). My colleague said that that was nonsense because no one can see God and live (Exodus 33:20). Not only Jacob, but many have seen God (Judges 13:22; 1 Kings 9:1-9; 1 Kings 22:19; Isaiah 6:1-2). He later reluctantly agreed with me.

Like most teenagers, I attended church with friends but did not read the Bible at home. In Church various aspects of Scripture were mentioned, but the worship service was more about ritual, tradition, and socializing than the Bible. Most of the religious lay persons I met attended church and went home. Those who were very religious were preoccupied with what their denominational beliefs were about and the requirements to be a member of their church. When I began to read the Bible, I found stories, particularly in the Old Testament, that were contrary to some messages delivered in church and not mentioned by anyone outside church. Not only did God contradict Himself, for instance, as to whether a brother must marry their brother's widow (Leviticus 20:21 versus Deuteronomy 25:5), and about killing anyone who sees Him as mentioned above, but He was inordinately cruel, even dictating ethnic cleansing as discussed in "Cruel in His Image." These stories and those of cannibalism, rape, incest, and adultery seem inappropriate for children and of little value for adult discussion. In contrast, the stories of Noah's ark and of Jonah in a fish seem appealing to children and remembered fondly by many adults. Most devout Christians know best only an edited version of the Bible and use camaraderie and denominational tradition as the avenue for spirituality and worship. To know the fourteen names of the original twelve apostles of Jesus is not a requisite to spirituality nor is knowing the name of the thirteenth apostle important for church membership. Special rules and beliefs define the Christian denomination, not biblical scholarship.

The requirement for church membership in some denominations is the belief that every word in the Bible is true. As with all beliefs, this one requires no objectivity, only acceptance. A great proponent of this position is Adrian Rogers, who is given much credit for ejecting moderate Baptists from the Southern Baptist Convention as president in 1979, 1986, and 1987 (CA 5/4/03). His Baptist church and religious complex serves 28,000 members, the largest in the USA, and is worth $80 million. They have erected huge freestanding crosses, at some expense, that may be seen for miles by motorists. Among his members are physicians, lawyers, teachers, business men, politicians, and all kinds of folk. His forte is oratory that he attributes to God. The Holy Ghost made him pastor of his church (CA 6/14/00). He asserts that the Bible account of Adam and Eve, Jonah and the fish, and all other biblical stories are facts of science and history (CA 5/4/03). Thus his followers must accept as fact that Samson's prodigious strength came with seven locks of hair (Judges 16:19, KJV) and not from sinew and testosterone. They must accept that Jotham recorded the words of bramble, trees, and vines talking (Judges 9:7–15) Likewise, the words of a female ass (donkey) complaining to her master Balaam have been recorded as perfect history and science (Numbers 22:28, 30). How many must accept as fact that Jesus said from heaven that he would kill the children of Jezebel (Revelations 2:23, KJV)? And the fact that Jesus said true believers "shall take up serpents; and if they drink any deadly thing, it shall not hurt them" (Mark 15:17-18) should humble any Christian who claims to be a true believer. In blissful ignorance, Rogers summarizes his knowledge of evolution as "monkey mythology" (CA 5/4/03). This is unfair to the scientists throughout the world who continue to discover fascinating evidence of early life on earth and unfair to the younger generation who are taught to hold such findings in contempt. It closes their minds to the facts of nature that many behold as God's wonders. For a preacher to dismiss scientific facts as monkey mythology is divine dishonesty. I believe that most Americans consider it wrong to denigrate the honest work of scientists.

Rogers and his ilk could take a lesson on Christian etiquette from Paul. He tells us that we have no right as Christians to criticize or look down on others (Romans 14:10, TLB). We are to love one another to fulfill the law (Romans 13:8, KJV). Even though we know that we are right with God, we must not flaunt our faith in front of others who might be hurt by it (Romans 14:22, TLB). Moreover, we must not do anything that will draw criticism to ourselves even though we know we are right (Romans 14:16, TLB). He also advises us to please our neighbors for their edification, just as Christ did not come to please himself (Romans 5:2-3). In short, we are to be civil to others and avoid any ostentatious display of our faith.

The poet Thomas Gray (1716–71) was apparently the first to use the words "ignorance is bliss." Will Rogers (1879–1935) made a point on the subject when he wrote, "You know everybody is ignorant, only on different subjects." The great Socrates (469–399 B.C.) was more humble when he wrote, "I know nothing except the fact of my ignorance." While Christopher Marlowe (1564–93) said ignorance was the only sin, David Mcculough indicated that it was at least shameful when he wrote in *Reader's Digest* (December 2002), "Indifference to history isn't just ignorance, it's a form of ingratitude." Certainly ignorance is not a virtue, but time and the limitations of the mind require, as Rogers thought, that we must be ignorant of something. Ignorance must be sinful, however, when facts of reality are ignored only because individuals of influence summarily declare them false. It has been said that some dismiss the Holocaust of WWII as a fabrication and in America witchcraft has been used to explain murder, as previously mentioned. It takes no effort to be ignorant, and in this it is bliss.

One thing seems certain, people are blissfully ignorant of the religions of others. L. Gordon Milton has compiled information on 2,630 faiths (CA 2/1/03) and the AARP *Modern Maturity* (September 2002) stated that there are 9,900 religions in the world but did not say who counted. In any case, there are thousands of faiths that influence mentation and attitude. Typically, followers are taught the symbolism of worship, but remain ignorant of the theology. That is left to the mullah, Brahman, preacher, priest, and other religious leaders to know best. Religion may be hurtful to its members. Hinduism, for instance, demands that followers adhere to the *Laws of Manu* that make millions unequal at birth for life. India has outlaw the caste system of Hinduism but the untouchables continue to be terribly abused (*National Geographic*, June 2003). Some of the 160 million untouchables fight for dignity and equality with violence because secular laws are rarely enforced. So, Hindus kill Hindus and the Brahman looks down at the great Mahatma Gandhi because he was only of the Vaisya caste (*National Geographic*, June 2003).

A caste or tribal mentality seems all too common to religion. Christians too often look down on Christians of a different sect, as do Moslems on Moslems. Arrogant leaders know that their religion is the only true one, foster derision, and proclaim religious tolerance to be devilry. But religions make nothing: not nails, toasters, clocks, automobiles, or airplanes. Farming, engineering, and science advance without religion. But secular achievement means little to the religious demigods who claim they speak for God and vociferously condemn the faiths and honest work of others, to the applause of millions. Fortunately, there are still millions of Americans who speak of God, follow the civil teachings of the New Testament, and applaud the good works of others regardless of faith. To our Founding Fathers religion was personal. They prayed, but did not use religion or religious rhetoric for political or social gain. Thomas Paine (1737–1809) captured the spirit of that era when he wrote, "My country is the world, and my religion is to do good." Goodness seems like a good idea for any religion.

ACKNOWLEDGMENTS

THE AUTHOR WISHES TO THANK HIS ELDER SON FOR EXAMINING THE MANUSCRIPT for any gross errors in history; his younger son for helpful discussions of science and theology; and his wife, who read it with dismay but supported its premise.

INDEX